Birds of
New Hampshire
& Vermont

Field Guide
by Stan Tekiela

Adventure Publications
Cambridge, Minnesota

To my wife, Katherine, and daughter, Abigail, with all my love

Acknowledgments

Many thanks to the National Wildlife Refuge System along with state and local agencies, both public and private, for stewarding lands that are critical to the many bird species we so love.

Edited by Sandy Livoti

Cover and Book design and illustrations by Jonathan Norberg

Range maps produced by Anthony Hertzel

Photo credits by photographer and page number:

Cover photo: Eastern Bluebird by Stan Tekiela
Kevin T. Karlson: 56, 74 (juvenile), 314 (female) **Maslowski Wildlife Productions**: 44 (female), 214 (female), 324 **Brian E. Small**: 214 (male), 296 (winter, juvenile), 298 (winter) **Stan Tekiela**: 22, 24, 26, 28 (both), 30, 32, 34, 36 (all), 38 (both), 40 (perching, soaring), 42 (all), 44 (male), 46 (male), 48, 50 (both), 52 (both), 54 (both), 58, 60, 62, 64, 66, 68 (both), 70, 72 (both), 74 (breeding), 76 (both), 78 (all), 80, 82, 84, 86, 88 (both), 90 (both), 92, 94 (both), 96, 98, 100 (both), 102, 104 (both), 106, 108, 110, 112, 114, 116, 118, 120, 122 (both), 124, 126 (both), 128 (both), 130, 132, 134, 136, 138, 140, 142 (all), 144, 146 (both), 148 (female, juvenile), 150, 152 (all), 154 (male, female), 156, 158, 160 (both), 162, 164 (both), 166, 168, 170 (both), 172 (both), 174 (both), 176, 178, 180 (both), 182 (both), 184 (both), 186, 188, 190, 192 (both), 194, 196, 198 (soaring), 200 (all), 202 (both), 204, 206, 208 (both), 210 (both), 212 (all), 214 (insets), 216, 218 (both), 220 (both), 222 (both), 224 (all), 226, 228, 230, 232, 234, 236 (both), 238, 240, 242 (both), 244, 246, 248, 250 (soaring, juvenile), 252, 254, 256 (perching, soaring), 258 (perching, in flight, juvenile), 260 (male, soaring), 262 (both), 264 (both), 266 (both), 268, 270, 272, 274, 276 (male, in flight), 278, 280, 282 (male, first-year male), 284 (male, yellow male), 286, 288, 290 (male), 292, 294 (female, in flight), 296 (breeding, in flight), 298 (breeding, in flight, juvenile), 300 (all), 302 (both), 304, 306 (all), 308 (male), 310, 312 (both), 314 (male, winter male), 316, 318, 320, 322, 326, 328 (female), 330 (all), 332 **Brian K. Wheeler**: 40 (juvenile), 154 (both juveniles), 198 (female), 256 (juvenile), 258 (in flight juvenile) **Jim Zipp**: 154 (in flight), 250 (perching), 308 (female)

To the best of the publisher's knowledge, all photos were of live birds. Some were photographed in a controlled condition.

10 9 8 7 6 5 4

Birds of New Hampshire and Vermont Field Guide
Copyright © 2016 by Stan Tekiela
Published by Adventure Publications, an imprint of AdventureKEEN
310 Garfield Street South, Cambridge, Minnesota 55008
(800) 678-7006
www.adventurepublications.net
Printed in China
ISBN 978-1-59193-640-4 (pbk.); ISBN 978-1-59193-660-2 (ebook)

TABLE OF CONTENTS

WHY WATCH BIRDS IN NEW HAMPSHIRE AND VERMONT?

Millions of people have discovered bird feeding. It's a simple and enjoyable way to bring the beauty of birds closer to your home. Watching birds at your feeder and listening to them sing their songs often leads to a lifetime pursuit of bird identification. The *Birds of New Hampshire and Vermont Field Guide* is for those who want to identify the common birds seen in New Hampshire and Vermont.

There are over 1,100 species of birds found in North America. In New Hampshire alone there have been more than 409 different kinds of birds recorded throughout the years, and in Vermont over 384 species have been reported. These are impressive numbers of species for two individual states! These bird sightings were diligently recorded by hundreds of bird watchers and became part of the official state records. From these valuable records, I've chosen 130 of the most common and easily seen birds of New Hampshire and Vermont to include in this book.

Bird watching, or birding, is one of the most popular activities in America. Its appeal in New Hampshire and Vermont is due, in part, to an unusually rich and abundant birdlife. Why are so many birds in these states? The main reasons are open space and diversity of habitat. While New Hampshire and Vermont combined cover around 18,900 square miles (48,950 sq. km), despite the small area, the region is a remarkable place to see a variety of birds due to its wide range of habitats.

The White Mountains of northern New Hampshire have a peak elevation of 6,288 feet (1,917 m). This mountain range is a good place to see Horned Larks and other wonderful birds. The New England Uplands, which covers most western and southern parts of New Hampshire, is a great place to see forest and woodland birds, including Baltimore Orioles. Shorebirds and other unique birds not found in other parts of the state can be seen in the coastal lowlands of southeastern New Hampshire.

The Green Mountains are Vermont's principal geographical feature. Extending from the Canadian border into Massachusetts, these mountains not only have the highest peaks in the state, but they are home to some of the most interesting birds, such as Ruffed Grouse and the Wild Turkey. The Vermont Piedmont, a narrow corridor of hills and valleys to the east of the Green Mountains, composes much of the rest of the state. This is a good place to see Red-tailed Hawks and other open country birds.

From the coastal lowlands to the mountains, New Hampshire and Vermont are some of the best places in North America to see an assortment of birds. Whether you watch hummingbirds at spring flowers, bluebirds nesting in summer, hawks migrating in fall or cardinals feeding in winter, you'll enjoy an exciting array of birds in your state all year long.

OBSERVE WITH A STRATEGY:
TIPS FOR IDENTIFYING BIRDS

Identifying birds isn't as difficult as you might think. By simply following a few basic strategies, you can increase your chances of successfully identifying most birds you see! One of the first and easiest things to do when you see a new bird is to note its color. (Also, since this book is organized by color, you will go right to that color section to find it.)

Next, note the size of the bird. A strategy to quickly estimate size is to select a small-, medium- and large-sized bird to use for reference. For example, most people are familiar with robins. A robin, measured from tip of the bill to tip of the tail, is 10 inches (25 cm) long. Using the robin as an example of a medium-sized bird, select two other birds, one smaller and one larger. Many people use a House Sparrow, at about 6 inches (15 cm), and an American Crow, about 18 inches (45 cm). When you see a bird that you don't know, you can quickly ask yourself, "Is it smaller than a robin, but larger than a sparrow?" When you look in your field guide to help identify your bird, you'll know it is roughly between 6-10 inches (15-25 cm) long. This will help to narrow your choices.

Next, note the size, shape and color of the bill. Is it long, short, thick, thin, pointed, blunt, curved or straight? Seed-eating birds, such as Northern Cardinals, have bills that are thick and strong enough to crack even the toughest seeds. Birds that sip nectar, such as Ruby-throated Hummingbirds, need long thin bills to reach deep into flowers. Hawks and owls tear their prey with very sharp, curving bills. Sometimes, just noting the bill shape can help you decide whether the bird is a woodpecker, sparrow, grosbeak, blackbird or bird of prey.

Next, take a look around and note the habitat in which you see the bird. Is it wading in a saltwater marsh? Walking along a riverbank or on the beach? Soaring in the sky? Is it perched high in the trees or hopping along the forest floor? Because of their preferences in diet and habitat, you will usually see robins hopping on the ground, but not often eating seeds at a feeder. Or you'll see a Blue Jay sitting on a tree branch, but not climbing headfirst down a tree trunk like a White-breasted Nuthatch.

Noticing what a bird is eating will give you another clue to help you identify that bird. Feeding is a big part of any bird's life. Fully one-third of all bird activity revolves around searching for and catching food, or actually eating. While birds don't always follow all the rules of what we think they eat, you can make some general assumptions. Northern Flickers, for instance, feed upon ants and other insects, so you wouldn't expect to see them visiting a backyard feeder. Some birds, such as Barn Swallows and Tree Swallows, feed upon flying insects and spend hours swooping and diving to catch a meal.

Sometimes you can identify a bird by the way it perches. Body posture can help you differentiate between an American Crow and a Red-tailed Hawk. American Crows lean forward over their feet on a branch, while hawks perch in a vertical position. Look for this the next time you see a large unidentified bird in a tree.

Birds in flight are often difficult to identify, but noting the size and shape of the wing will help. A bird's wing size is in direct proportion to its body size, weight and type of flying. The shape of the wing determines if the bird flies fast and with precision, or slowly and less precisely. Birds such as House Finches, which flit around in thick tangles of branches, have short, round wings. Birds that soar on warm updrafts of air, such as Turkey Vultures, have long, broad wings. Barn Swallows have short, pointed wings that slice through the air, propelling their swift and accurate flight.

Some birds have unique patterns of flight that aid in identification. American Goldfinches fly in a distinctive up-and-down pattern that makes it look as if they are riding a roller coaster.

While it's not easy to make these observations in the short time you often have to watch a "mystery bird," practicing these methods of identification will greatly expand your skills in birding. Also, seek the guidance of a more experienced birder who will help you improve your skills and answer questions on the spot.

BIRD BASICS

It's easier to identify birds and communicate about them if you know the names of the different parts of a bird. For instance, it's more effective to use the word "crest" to indicate the set of extra-long feathers on top of a Northern Cardinal's head than to try to describe it.

The following illustration points out the basic parts of a bird. Because it's a composite of many birds, it shouldn't be confused with any actual bird.

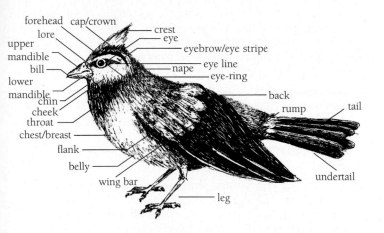

forehead cap/crown
lore
upper
mandible
bill
lower
mandible
chin
cheek
throat
chest/breast
flank
belly
wing bar

crest
eye
eyebrow/eye stripe
eye line
nape
eye-ring
back
rump
tail
undertail
leg

Bird Color Variables

No other animal has a color palette like a bird's. Brilliant blues, lemon yellows, showy reds and iridescent greens are commonplace within the bird world. In general, the male birds are more colorful than their female counterparts. This is probably to help the male attract a mate, essentially saying, "Hey, look at me!" It also calls attention to the male's overall health. The better the condition of his feathers, the better his food source and territory, and therefore the better his potential for a mate.

Female birds that don't look like their male counterparts (such species are called sexually dimorphic, meaning "two forms") are often a nondescript color, as seen in Indigo Buntings. These muted tones help hide the females during weeks of motionless incubation, and draw less attention to them when they are out feeding or taking a break from the rigors of raising their young.

In some species, such as the Bald Eagle, Blue Jay and Downy Woodpecker, male birds look nearly identical to the females. In the case of woodpeckers, the sexes are differentiated by only a single red mark or sometimes a yellow mark. Depending upon the species, the mark may be on top of the head, face, nape of neck or just behind the bill.

During the first year, juvenile birds often look like the mothers. Since brightly colored feathers are used mainly for attracting a mate, young non-breeding males don't have a need for colorful plumage. It is not until the first spring molt (or several years later, depending on the species) that young males obtain their breeding colors.

Both breeding and winter plumages are the result of molting. Molting is the process of dropping old worn feathers and replacing them with new ones. All birds molt, typically twice a year, with the spring molt usually occurring in late winter. During this time, most birds produce their breeding plumage (brighter colors for attracting mates), which lasts throughout the summer.

Winter plumage is the result of the late summer molt, which serves a couple of important functions. First, it adds feathers for warmth in the coming winter season. Second, in some species it produces feathers that tend to be drab in color, which helps to camouflage the birds and hide them from predators. The winter plumage of the male American Goldfinch, for example, is olive brown unlike its obvious canary yellow color during summer. Luckily for us, some birds, such as the male Northern Cardinal, retain their bright summer colors all year long.

Bird Nests

Bird nests are truly an amazing feat of engineering. Imagine building your home strong enough to weather a storm, large enough to hold your entire family, insulated enough to shelter them from cold and heat, and waterproof enough to keep out rain. Now, build it without any blueprints or directions, and without the use of your hands or feet! Birds do!

Before building a nest, an appropriate site must be selected. In some species, such as House Wrens, the male picks out several potential sites and assembles several small twigs in each. This discourages other birds from using nearby nest cavities. These "extra" nests are occasionally called dummy nests. The female is then taken around and shown all the choices. She chooses her favorite and finishes constructing the nest. In some other species of birds–Baltimore Orioles, for example–it is the female who chooses the site and constructs the nest, with the male offering only an occasional suggestion. Each species has its own nest-building routine, which is strictly followed.

As you'll see in the following illustrations, birds build a wide variety of nest types.

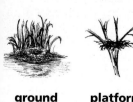

| ground nest | platform nest | cup nest | pendulous nest | cavity nest |

Nesting material often consists of natural elements found in the immediate area. Most nests consist of plant fibers (such as bark peeled from grapevines), sticks, mud, dried grass, feathers, fur, or soft fuzzy tufts from thistle. Some birds, including Ruby-throated Hummingbirds, use spider webs to glue nest materials together. Nesting material is limited to what a bird can hold or carry. Because of this, a bird must make many trips afield to gather enough materials to complete its nest. Most nests take at least four days or more, and hundreds, if not thousands, of trips to build.

The simple **ground nest** is scraped out of the earth. A shallow depression that usually contains no nesting material, it is made by birds such as the Killdeer and Horned Lark.

Another kind of nest, the **platform nest**, represents a more complex type of nest building. Constructed of small twigs and branches, the platform nest is a simple arrangement of sticks which forms a platform and features a small depression to nestle the eggs.

Some platform nests, such as those of the Canada Goose, are constructed on the ground and are made with mud and grass. Platform nests can also be on cliffs, bridges, balconies or even in flowerpots. This kind of nest gives space to adventurous youngsters and functions as a landing platform for the parents. Many waterfowl build platform nests on the ground, usually near water or actually in water. These floating platform nests vary with the water level, thus preventing nests with eggs from being flooded. Platform nests, constructed by such birds as Mourning Doves and herons, are not anchored to the tree and may tumble from the branches during high winds and storms.

The **cup nest** is a modified platform nest, used by three-quarters of all songbirds. Constructed from the outside in, a supporting platform is constructed first. This platform is attached firmly to a tree, shrub, rock ledge or the ground. Next, the sides are constructed of grasses, small twigs, bark or leaves, which are woven together and often glued with mud for added strength. The inner cup, lined with feathers, animal fur, soft plant material or animal hair, is constructed last. The mother bird uses her chest to cast the final contours of the inner nest.

The **pendulous nest** is an unusual nest, looking more like a sock hanging from a branch than a nest. Inaccessible to most predators, these nests are attached to the end of the smallest branches of a tree and often wave wildly in the breeze. Woven very tightly of plant fibers, they are strong, watertight and take up to a week to construct. More commonly used by tropical birds, this complicated type of nest has also been mastered by orioles and kinglets. A small opening on the top or side allows the parents access to the grass-lined interior. (It must be one heck of a ride to be inside one of these nests during a windy spring thunderstorm!)

Another type of nest, the **cavity nest**, is used by many bird species, including woodpeckers and Eastern Bluebirds. The cavity nest is usually excavated in a tree branch or trunk and offers shelter from storms, sun, predators and cold. A relatively small entrance hole in a tree leads to an inner chamber up to 10 inches (25 cm) deep. Usually constructed by woodpeckers, the cavity nest is typically used only once by its builder but subsequently can be used for many years by other birds, such as mergansers, bluebirds and swallows, which do not have the capability of excavating one for themselves. Kingfishers, on the other hand, excavate a tunnel up to 4 feet (1 m) long, which connects the entrance in a riverbank to the nest chamber. These cavity nests are often sparsely lined because they are already well insulated.

One of the most clever of all nest types is known as the **no nest** or daycare nest. Parasitic birds, such as Brown-headed Cowbirds, build no nests at all! The egg-laden female expertly searches out other birds' nests and sneaks in to lay one of her own eggs while the host mother is not looking, thereby leaving the host mother to raise an adopted youngster. The mother cowbird wastes no energy building a nest only to have it raided by a predator. By using several nests of other birds, she spreads out her progeny so at least one of her offspring will live to maturity.

Some birds, including some swallows, take nest building one step further. They use a collection of small balls of mud to construct an adobe-style home. Constructed beneath the eaves of houses, under bridges or inside chimneys, some of these nests look like simple cup nests. Others are completely enclosed, with small tunnel-like openings that lead into a safe nesting chamber for the baby birds.

Who Builds the Nest?

In general, the female bird builds the nest. She gathers nesting materials and constructs a nest, with an occasional visit from her mate to check on progress. In some species, both parents contribute equally to the construction of a nest. A male bird might forage for precisely the right sticks, grass or mud, but it is often the female that forms or puts together the nest. She uses her body to form the egg chamber. Rarely does the male build a nest by himself.

Fledging

Fledging is the interval between hatching and flight or leaving the nest. Some birds leave the nest within hours of hatching (precocial), but it might be weeks before they are able to fly. This is common with waterfowl and shorebirds. Until they start to fly, they are called fledglings. Birds that are still in the nest are called nestlings. Other baby birds are born naked and blind, and remain in the nest for several weeks (altricial).

Why Birds Migrate

Why do birds migrate? The short answer is simple–food. Birds migrate to areas with high concentrations of food, as it is easier to breed where food is than where it is not. A typical migrating bird–the Purple Martin, for instance–will migrate from the tropics of South America to nest in forests of North America, taking advantage of billions of newly hatched insects to feed its young. This trip is called **complete migration**.

Some birds of prey return from their complete migration to northern regions that are overflowing with small rodents, such as mice and voles, that have continued to breed in winter.

Complete migrators have a set time and pattern of migration. Each year at nearly the same time, they take off and head for a specific wintering ground. Complete migrators may travel great distances, sometimes as much as 15,000 miles (24,150 km) or more in one year. But complete migration does not necessarily imply flying from the frozen northland to a tropical destination. American Tree Sparrow, for example, is a complete migrator that flies from Canada to spend the winter in New Hampshire and Vermont. This is still called **complete migration**.

There are many interesting aspects to complete migrators. In the spring, males usually migrate several weeks before the females, arriving early to scope out possibilities for nesting sites and food sources, and to begin to defend territories. The females arrive several weeks later. In the autumn, in many species, the females and their young leave early, often up to four weeks before the adult males.

All migrators are not the same type. **Partial migrators**, such as American Goldfinches, usually wait until their food supplies dwindle before flying south. Unlike complete migrators, partial migrators move only far enough south, or sometimes east and west, to find abundant food. In some years it might be only a few hundred miles, while in other years it might be nearly a thousand. This kind of migration, dependent on weather and the availability of food, is sometimes called seasonal movement.

Unlike the predictable ebbing and flowing behavior of complete migrators or partial migrators, **irruptive migrators** can move every third to fifth year or, in some cases, in consecutive years. These migrations are triggered when times are really tough and food is scarce. Pine Grosbeaks are a good example of irruptive migrators, because they leave their normal northern range in search of food or in response to overpopulation.

How Do Birds Migrate?

One of the many secrets of migration is fat. While we humans are fighting the battle of the bulge, birds intentionally gorge themselves to put on as much fat as possible while still being able to fly. Fat provides the greatest amount of energy per unit of weight, and in the same way that your car needs gas, birds are propelled by fat and stalled without it.

During long migratory flights, fat deposits are used up quickly, and birds need to stop to "refuel." This is when backyard bird feeding stations and undeveloped, natural spaces around our towns and cities are especially important. Some birds require up to 2-3 days of constant feeding to build their fat reserves before continuing their seasonal trip.

Some birds, such as most eagles, hawks, ospreys, falcons and vultures, migrate during the day. Larger birds can hold more body fat, go longer without eating and take longer to migrate. These birds glide along on rising columns of warm air, called thermals, which hold them aloft while they slowly make their way north or south. They generally rest during the night and hunt early in the morning before the sun has a chance to warm the land and create good soaring conditions. Birds migrating during the day use a combination of landforms, rivers, and the rising and setting sun to guide them in the right direction.

Most other birds migrate during the night. Studies show that some birds which migrate at night use the stars to navigate. Others use the setting sun, while still others, such as doves, use the earth's magnetic fields to guide them north or south. While flying at night might seem like a crazy idea, nocturnal migration is safer for several reasons. First, there are fewer nighttime predators for migrating birds. Second, traveling at night allows time during the day to find food in unfamiliar surroundings. Finally, nighttime wind patterns tend to be flat, or laminar. These flat winds don't have the turbulence associated with daytime winds and can actually help carry smaller birds by pushing them along.

HOW TO USE THIS GUIDE

To help you quickly and easily identify birds, this field guide is organized by color. Simply note the color of the bird and turn to that section. Refer to the first page for the color key. The Pileated Woodpecker, for example, is black and white with a red crest. Because this bird is mostly black and white, it will be found in the black and white section. Each color section is also arranged by size, generally with the smaller birds first. Sections may also incorporate the average size in a range, which, in some cases, reflects size differences between male and female birds. Flip through the pages in that color section to find the bird. If you already know the name of the bird, check the index for the page number. In some species, the male and female are remarkably different in color. In others, the color of breeding and winter plumages differs. These species will have an inset photograph with a page reference and, in most cases, are found in two color sections.

In the description section you will find a variety of information about the bird. On page 21 is a sample of information included in the book.

Range Maps

Range maps are included for each bird. Colored areas indicate where in New Hampshire and Vermont a particular bird is most likely to be found. The colors represent the presence of a species during a specific season, not the density or amount of birds in the area. Green is used for summer, blue for winter, red for year-round and yellow for areas where the bird is seen during migration. While every effort has been made to accurately depict these ranges, they are only general guidelines. Ranges actually change on an ongoing basis due to a variety of factors. Changes in weather, species abundance, landscape and vital resources, such as availability of food and water, can affect local populations, migration and movements, causing birds to be found in areas that are atypical for the species.

Colored areas simply mean bird sightings for that species have been frequent in those areas and less frequent in others. Please use the maps as intended–as general guides only.

Common Name

YEAR-ROUND
MIGRATION
SUMMER
WINTER

Range Map — *Scientific name* — **Color Indicator** —

Size: measures head to tail, may include wingspan

Male: a brief description of the male bird, and may include breeding, winter or other plumages

Female: a brief description of the female bird, which is sometimes not the same as the male

Juvenile: a brief description of the juvenile bird, which often looks like the female

Nest: the kind of nest this bird builds to raise its young; who builds the nest; how many broods per year

Eggs: how many eggs you might expect to see in a nest; color and marking

Incubation: the average time parents spend incubating the eggs; who does the incubation

Fledging: the average time young spend in the nest after hatching but before they leave the nest; who does the most "childcare" and feeding

Migration: complete (consistent, seasonal), partial (seasonal movement, destination varies), irruptive (unpredictable, depends on the food supply), non-migrator; additional comments

Food: what the bird eats most of the time (e.g., seeds, insects, fruit, nectar, small mammals, fish); if it typically comes to a bird feeding station

Compare: notes about other birds that look similar, and the pages on which they can be found, may include extra information to help identify

Stan's Notes: Interesting gee-whiz natural history information. This could be something to look or listen for, or something to help positively identify the bird. Also includes remarkable features.

male

female
pg. 323

Bobolink
Dolichonyx oryzivorus

SUMMER

Size: 7" (18 cm)

Male: Nearly all-black bird with a black chest and belly. Pale yellow on back of head and nape of neck. White patch on wings and rump.

Female: pale yellow with dark brown stripes on the head, thin dark line extends through the eye, dark streaks on back and sides

Juvenile: similar to female, lacking dark streaks

Nest: ground; scraped-out depression lined with grass; 1 brood per year

Eggs: 4-6; gray to red brown with brown markings

Incubation: 10-13 days; female incubates

Fledging: 10-14 days; female and male feed young

Migration: complete, to South America, mostly Brazil

Food: insects, seeds

Compare: Male Bobolink is similar in size to the male Red-winged Blackbird (pg. 31), but lacks the red and yellow wing bars. Look for yellow on the head, a white patch on the wings and the black belly of male Bobolink.

Stan's Notes: A member of the blackbird family. Closely related to meadowlarks. A common bird of prairies, grasslands and open fields. In spring, the male will perch on plant stems and repeat its bubbling "bob-o-link" song (which provided the common name). Gives a loud, repeated "ink" whistle during flight. When disturbed, the female will run from her highly concealed ground nest before taking flight. By late summer, the males will have molted to a drab color similar to the females.

female pg. 139

male

Eastern Towhee
Pipilo erythrophthalmus

Size: 7-8" (18-20 cm)

Male: Mostly black with dirty red brown sides and a white belly. Long black tail with a white tip. Short, stout, pointed bill and rich red eyes. White wing patches flash in flight.

Female: similar to male, but is brown, not black

Juvenile: light brown with heavily streaked head, chest and belly, long dark tail with a white tip

Nest: cup; female builds; 2 broods per year

Eggs: 3-4; creamy white with brown markings

Incubation: 12-13 days; female incubates

Fledging: 10-12 days; male and female feed young

Migration: complete, to southern states, South America

Food: insects, seeds, fruit; visits ground feeders

Compare: Slightly smaller than the American Robin (pg. 243), which lacks the white belly. The Gray Catbird (pg. 241) lacks the black head and rusty sides. Common Grackle (pg. 33) lacks a white belly and has a long thin bill. Male Rose-breasted Grosbeak (pg. 49) has a rosy patch in the center of its chest.

Stan's Notes: Common name comes from its distinctive "tow-hee" call given by both sexes. Mostly known for its characteristic call that sounds like, "Drink-your-tea!" Seen hopping backward with both feet (bilateral scratching), raking up leaf litter for insects and seeds. The female broods, but the male does most of the feeding of young. In southern coastal states, some have red eyes; others have white eyes. The red-eyed variety is seen in New Hampshire and Vermont.

female
pg. 141

male

Brown-headed Cowbird
Molothrus ater

YEAR-ROUND
SUMMER

Size: 7½" (19 cm)

Male: Glossy black bird, reminiscent of a male Red-winged Blackbird. Head is chocolate brown. Pointed, sharp gray bill. Dark eyes.

Female: dull brown bird, bill similar to the male bill

Juvenile: similar to female, but dull gray color and has a streaked chest

Nest: no nest; lays eggs in the nests of other birds

Eggs: 5-7; white with brown markings

Incubation: 10-13 days; host bird incubates eggs

Fledging: 10-11 days; host birds feed young

Migration: partial to non-migrator in New Hampshire and Vermont

Food: insects, seeds; will come to seed feeders

Compare: The male Red-winged Blackbird (pg. 31) is slightly larger with red and yellow patches on upper wings. Common Grackle (pg. 33) has a long tail and lacks the brown head. European Starling (pg. 29) has a shorter tail.

Stan's Notes: Member of the blackbird family. Of approximately 750 species of parasitic birds worldwide, this is the only parasitic bird in New Hampshire and Vermont, laying eggs in host birds' nests, leaving others to raise its young. Cowbirds are known to have laid eggs in the nests of over 200 species of birds. Some birds reject cowbird eggs, but most will incubate them and raise the young, even to the exclusion of their own. Look for warblers and other birds feeding young birds twice their own size. At one time cowbirds followed bison to feed on insects attracted to the animals.

winter

breeding

European Starling
Sturnus vulgaris

Size: 7½" (19 cm)

Male: Gray-to-black bird with white speckles in fall and winter. Shiny purple black during spring and summer. Long, pointed yellow bill in spring turns gray in fall. Short tail.

Female: same as male

Juvenile: similar to adult, gray brown in color with a streaked chest

Nest: cavity; male and female line cavity; 2 broods per year

Eggs: 4-6; bluish with brown markings

Incubation: 12-14 days; female and male incubate

Fledging: 18-20 days; female and male feed young

Migration: non-migrator to partial; some will move to southern states

Food: insects, seeds, fruit; will come to seed and suet feeders

Compare: Similar to Common Grackle (pg. 33), but lacks its long tail. The male Brown-headed Cowbird (pg. 27) is the same size, but it has a brown head and longer tail.

Stan's Notes: A great songster, this bird can mimic other birds and sounds. Often displaces woodpeckers, chickadees and other cavity-nesting birds. Can be very aggressive and destroy eggs or young of other birds. Jaws are designed to be the most powerful when opening; the birds can pry crevices apart to locate hidden insects. Bill changes color with the seasons: yellow in spring, gray in autumn. Gathers in the hundreds in autumn. Not a native bird, it was introduced to New York City in 1890-91 from Europe.

female
pg. 151

male

Red-winged Blackbird
Agelaius phoeniceus

YEAR-ROUND SUMMER

Size: 8½" (22 cm)

Male: Jet-black bird with red and yellow shoulder patches on upper wings. Pointed black bill.

Female: heavily streaked brown bird with a pointed brown bill and white eyebrows

Juvenile: same as female

Nest: cup; female builds; 2-3 broods per year

Eggs: 3-4; bluish green with brown markings

Incubation: 10-12 days; female incubates

Fledging: 11-14 days; female and male feed young

Migration: complete, to southeastern New Hampshire, southern states, Mexico and Central America

Food: seeds, insects; will come to seed feeders

Compare: Slightly larger than the male Brown-headed Cowbird (pg. 27), but is less iridescent and lacks the Cowbird's brown head. Differs from all other blackbirds due to the red and yellow patches on its wings (epaulets).

Stan's Notes: One of the most widespread and numerous birds in New Hampshire and Vermont. It's a sure sign of spring when these birds return to the marshes. Flocks with as many as 10,000 birds have been reported. Males arrive before females and defend their territories by singing from the top of surrounding vegetation. Male repeats his call from cattail tops while showing off his red and yellow shoulder patches. Female chooses a mate and often nests over shallow water in thick stands of cattails. Can be aggressive when defending the nest. Feeds mostly on seeds in fall and spring, switching to insects in summer.

YEAR-ROUND
SUMMER

Common Grackle
Quiscalus quiscula

Size:	11-13" (28-33 cm)
Male:	Large black bird with an iridescent blue black head, a purple brown body, long black tail, long thin bill and bright golden eyes.
Female:	similar to male, only duller and smaller
Juvenile:	similar to female
Nest:	cup; female builds; 2 broods per year
Eggs:	4-5; greenish white with brown markings
Incubation:	13-14 days; female incubates
Fledging:	16-20 days; female and male feed young
Migration:	complete to partial migrator in New Hampshire and Vermont; moves around in search of food
Food:	fruit, seeds, insects; comes to seed feeders
Compare:	European Starling (pg. 29) is much smaller with a speckled appearance, and has a yellow bill during breeding season. Male Red-winged Blackbird (pg. 31) has red and yellow wing markings (epaulets).

Stan's Notes: Usually nests in small colonies of up to 75 pairs but travels with other blackbird species in large flocks. Known to feed in farmers' fields. The common name is derived from the Latin word *graculus*, meaning "to cough," for its loud raspy call. Male holds tail in a deep V shape during flight. The flight pattern is usually level, as opposed to an undulating up-and-down movement. Unlike most birds, it has larger muscles for opening the mouth (rather than for closing it) and prying crevices apart to locate hidden insects.

American Coot
Fulica americana

Size: 13-16" (33-40 cm)

Male: Slate gray to black all over. White bill with a dark band near the tip. Green legs and feet. A small white patch near the base of the tail. Prominent red eyes. A small red patch above the bill between the eyes.

Female: same as male

Juvenile: much paler than adult, with a gray bill and same white rump patch

Nest: floating platform; female and male build; 1 brood per year

Eggs: 9-12; pinkish buff with brown markings

Incubation: 21-25 days; female and male incubate

Fledging: 49-52 days; female and male feed young

Migration: complete, to southern states, Mexico and Central America

Food: insects, aquatic plants

Compare: Smaller than most other waterfowl. This is the only black water bird or duck-like bird with a white bill.

Stan's Notes: An excellent diver and swimmer, typically seen in large flocks on open water. Not a duck, as it doesn't have webbed feet, but instead has large lobed toes. When taking off, scrambles across the surface of water with wings flapping. Bobs head while swimming. Anchors its floating nest to plants. Huge flocks of up to 1,000 birds gather for migration. The unusual common name "Coot" is of unknown origin, but in Middle English, the word *coote* was used to describe various waterfowl–perhaps it stuck. Also called Mud Hen. A favorite food of Bald Eagles.

Fish Crow

in flight

American Crow
Corvus brachyrhynchos

Size: 18" (45 cm)

Male: All-black bird with black bill, legs and feet. Can have a purple sheen in direct sunlight.

Female: same as male

Juvenile: same as adult

Nest: platform; female builds; 1 brood per year

Eggs: 4-6; bluish to olive green with brown marks

Incubation: 18 days; female incubates

Fledging: 28-35 days; female and male feed young

Migration: non-migrator to partial

Food: fruit, insects, mammals, fish, carrion; will come to seed and suet feeders

Compare: The Common Raven (pg. 39) has a larger bill, shaggy throat feathers and a deep, raspy call. Raven has a wedge-shaped tail, apparent in flight; American Crow has a squared tail. Fish Crow (see inset) is strikingly similar, but the American is larger, has a shorter tail, larger head and bill, and a lower-pitched call.

Stan's Notes: A familiar bird. Often reuses its nest every year if not taken over by a Great Horned Owl. Collects and stores bright, shiny objects in the nest. Mimics other birds and human voices. One of the smartest of all birds and very social, often entertaining itself by provoking chases with other birds. Eats roadkill but rarely hit by vehicles. May live up to 20 years. Unmated birds, called helpers, help raise the young. Large extended families roost together at night, dispersing daily to hunt. American and Fish Crows are best distinguished by their remarkably different calls. The American gives a harsh "caw"; the Fish gives a nasal, high-pitched "cah."

in flight

Common Raven
Corvus corax

YEAR-ROUND

Size: 22-27" (56-69 cm)

Male: Large all-black bird with a large black bill, a shaggy beard of feathers on the throat and chin, and a large wedge-shaped tail, as seen in flight.

Female: same as male

Juvenile: same as adult

Nest: platform; female and male construct; 1 brood per year

Eggs: 4-6; pale green with brown markings

Incubation: 18-21 days; female incubates

Fledging: 38-44 days; female and male feed young

Migration: non-migrator; moves around to find food

Food: insects, fruit, small animals, carrion

Compare: Larger than its cousin, the American Crow (pg. 37), which lacks shaggy throat feathers. Glides on flat, outstretched wings unlike the slight V-shaped wing pattern of the American Crow. Listen for the Raven's deep, low raspy call to distinguish it from the higher-pitched American Crow.

Stan's Notes: Considered by some people to be the smartest of all birds. Known for its aerial acrobatics and long swooping dives. Sometimes scavenges with crows and gulls. A cooperative hunter that often communicates the location of a good source of food to other ravens. Complex courtship includes grabbing bills, preening each other and cooing. Most begin to breed at 3-4 years. Mates are long-term. Uses the same nest site for many years.

soaring

juvenile

Turkey Vulture
Cathartes aura

SUMMER

Size: 26-32" (66-80 cm); up to 6-foot wingspan

Male: Large bird with an obvious red head and legs. In flight, the wings appear two-toned: black leading edge with gray on the trailing edge and tip. The tips of wings end in finger-like projections. Long squared tail. Ivory bill.

Female: same as male

Juvenile: similar to adult, with a gray-to-blackish head and bill

Nest: no nest, or minimal nest on a cliff or in a cave; 1 brood per year

Eggs: 1-3; white with brown markings

Incubation: 38-41 days; female and male incubate

Fledging: 66-88 days; female and male feed young

Migration: complete, to southern states, Mexico and Central and South America

Food: carrion; parents regurgitate for young

Compare: Bald Eagle (pg. 79) is larger and lacks two-toned wings. Unlike the Bald Eagle, Turkey Vulture holds its wings in a slight V shape during flight.

Stan's Notes: The vulture's naked head is an adaptation to reduce risk of feather fouling (picking up diseases) from carcasses. Unlike hawks and eagles, it has weak feet more suited to walking than grasping. One of the few birds that has a developed sense of smell. Mostly mute, making only grunts and groans. Seen in trees with wings outstretched, sunning itself.

in flight

juvenile

crests

drying

Double-crested Cormorant
Phalacrocorax auritus

MIGRATION
SUMMER

Size: 33" (84 cm); up to 4⅓-foot wingspan

Male: Large black water bird with a long snake-like neck. Long gray bill with yellow at the base and a hooked tip.

Female: same as male

Juvenile: lighter brown with a grayish chest and neck

Nest: platform, in a colony; male and female build; 1 brood per year

Eggs: 3-4; bluish white without markings

Incubation: 25-29 days; female and male incubate

Fledging: 37-42 days; male and female feed young

Migration: complete, to southern states, Mexico and Central America

Food: small fish, aquatic insects

Compare: Turkey Vulture (pg. 41) is similar in size and also perches on branches with wings open to dry in the sun, but it has a naked red head. American Coot (pg. 35) lacks the long neck and long pointed bill.

Stan's Notes: Often seen flying in a large V formation. Usually roosts in large groups in trees near water. Swims underwater to catch fish, holding its wings at its sides. Lacks the oil gland that keeps feathers from becoming waterlogged. To dry off, it strikes an erect pose with wings outstretched, facing the sun. The common name refers to the two crests on its head, which are not usually seen. "Cormorant" comes from the Latin words *corvus*, meaning "crow," and *L. marinus*, meaning "pertaining to the sea," literally, "Sea Crow."

43

male

female

SUMMER

Black-and-white Warbler
Mniotilta varia

Size: 5" (13 cm)

Male: Striped like a zebra, this small warbler has a distinctive black-and-white striped crown. White belly. Black chin and cheek patch.

Female: same as male, only duller and without the black chin and cheek patch

Juvenile: similar to female

Nest: cup; female builds; 1 brood per year

Eggs: 4-5; white with brown markings

Incubation: 10-11 days; female incubates

Fledging: 9-12 days; female and male feed young

Migration: complete, to Florida, Mexico and Central and South America

Food: insects

Compare: Like the White-breasted Nuthatch (pg. 223) and Red-breasted Nuthatch (pg. 219), look for Black-and-white Warbler to creep down tree trunks headfirst.

Stan's Notes: This is the only warbler that moves headfirst down tree trunks. Look for it searching for insect eggs in the bark of large trees. Its song sounds like a slowly turning, squeaky wheel going round and round. Female performs a distraction dance to draw predators away from the nest. Constructs its nest on the ground, concealing it under dead leaves or at the base of a tree. Found in a variety of habitats.

male

female

Downy Woodpecker
Dryobates pubescens

YEAR-ROUND

Size: 6" (15 cm)

Male: A small woodpecker with an all-white belly, black-and-white spotted wings, a black line running through the eyes, a short black bill, a white stripe down the back and red mark on the back of the head. Several small black spots along the sides of white tail.

Female: same as male, but lacks a red mark on head

Juvenile: same as female, some have a red mark near the forehead

Nest: cavity; male and female excavate; 1 brood per year

Eggs: 3-5; white without markings

Incubation: 11-12 days; female and male incubate, female incubates during the day, male at night

Fledging: 20-25 days; male and female feed young

Migration: non-migrator

Food: insects, seeds; visits seed and suet feeders

Compare: Nearly identical to the Hairy Woodpecker (pg. 53), but smaller. Look for the shorter, thinner bill to help identify the Downy.

Stan's Notes: Abundant and widespread where trees are present, and perhaps the most common woodpecker in the United States. Stiff tail feathers help brace it like a tripod as it clings to a tree. Like other woodpeckers, it has a long, barbed tongue to pull insects from tiny places. Male and female drum on branches or hollow logs to announce territory, which is rarely larger than 5 acres (2 ha). Male performs most of the brooding. Will winter roost in cavity.

47

female pg. 137

male

Rose-breasted Grosbeak
Pheucticus ludovicianus

SUMMER

Size: 7-8" (18-20 cm)

Male: A plump black-and-white bird with a large, triangular rose patch in the center of chest. Wing linings are rosy red. Large ivory bill.

Female: heavily streaked brown and white bird, large white eyebrows, orange yellow wing linings

Juvenile: similar to female

Nest: cup; female and male construct; 1-2 broods per year

Eggs: 3-5; blue green with brown markings

Incubation: 13-14 days; female and male incubate

Fledging: 9-12 days; female and male feed young

Migration: complete, to Mexico, Central America and South America

Food: insects, seeds, fruit; comes to seed feeders

Compare: Male is very distinctive with no look-alikes.

Stan's Notes: Seen in small groups throughout New Hampshire and Vermont during spring and migration. Often prefers a mature deciduous forest for nesting. Both sexes sing, but the male sings much louder and clearer. Sings a rich, robin-like song. Common name "Grosbeak" refers to its large bill, used to crush seeds. Rose breast patch varies in size and shape in each male. Males have white wing patches that flash in flight. Males arrive at their destinations first, joined by the females several days later. Several will come to seed feeders at the same time during spring. When the females arrive, males become territorial and reduce their visits to feeders. Young grosbeaks visit feeders with the adults after fledging.

male

female

Yellow-bellied Sapsucker
Sphyrapicus varius

MIGRATION
SUMMER

Size: 8-9" (20-22.5 cm)

Male: Medium-sized woodpecker with a checkered back. Red forehead, crown and chin. Tan-to-yellow breast and belly. White wing patches flash while flying.

Female: similar to male, white chin

Juvenile: similar to female, dull brown and lacks any red marking

Nest: cavity; female and male excavate; 1 brood per year

Eggs: 5-6; white without markings

Incubation: 12-13 days; female and male incubate, female incubates during the day, male at night

Fledging: 25-29 days; female and male feed young

Migration: complete, to southern states, Mexico and Central America

Food: insects, tree sap; comes to suet feeders

Compare: Similar to other woodpeckers, but the male is the only woodpecker in New Hampshire and Vermont with a red chin. Female Yellow-bellied has a white chin.

Stan's Notes: Drills holes in a pattern of horizontal rows in small-to medium-sized trees to bleed tree sap. Many birds drink from the sapsucker taps. Oozing sap also attracts insects, which sapsuckers eat. Sapsuckers will defend their sapping sites from the other birds. They don't suck sap; rather, they lap it with their long tongues. A quiet bird with few vocalizations, but will mew like a cat. Unlike other woodpeckers, drumming rhythm is irregular.

51

male

female

YEAR-ROUND

Hairy Woodpecker
Dryobates villosus

Size: 9" (22.5 cm)

Male: A black-and-white woodpecker with a white belly. Black wings with rows of white spots. White stripe down the back. Long black bill. Red mark on back of head.

Female: same as male, but lacks a red mark on head

Juvenile: grayer version of female

Nest: cavity; female and male excavate; 1 brood per year

Eggs: 3-6; white without markings

Incubation: 11-15 days; female and male incubate, female incubates during the day, male at night

Fledging: 28-30 days; male and female feed young

Migration: non-migrator

Food: insects, nuts, seeds; will come to seed and suet feeders

Compare: Larger than the Downy Woodpecker (pg. 47) and has a longer bill that is nearly the width of its head.

Stan's Notes: A common woodpecker of wooded backyards that announces its arrival with a sharp chirp before landing on feeders. This bird is responsible for eating many destructive forest insects. Has a barbed tongue, which helps it extract insects from trees. Tiny bristle-like feathers at the base of bill protect the nostrils from wood dust. Drums on hollow logs, branches or stovepipes in spring to announce its territory. Often prefers to excavate nest cavities in live aspen trees. Has a larger, more oval-shaped cavity entrance than that of the Downy Woodpecker.

male

female

YEAR-ROUND

Red-bellied Woodpecker
Melanerpes carolinus

Size: 9¼" (23 cm)

Male: "Zebra-backed" woodpecker with a white rump. Red crown extends down the nape of neck. Tan breast with a tinge of red on belly, which is often hard to see.

Female: same as male, but has a light gray crown and red nape

Juvenile: gray version of adults, lacks a red crown and red nape

Nest: cavity; female and male excavate; 1 brood per year

Eggs: 4-5; white without markings

Incubation: 12-14 days; female and male incubate, female incubates during the day, male at night

Fledging: 24-27 days; female and male feed young

Migration: non-migrator; moves around to find food

Food: insects, nuts, fruit; visits seed and suet feeders

Compare: Similar to the Northern Flicker (pg. 161) and Yellow-bellied Sapsucker (pg. 51). Note the tan chest and belly with obvious black-and-white stripes on the back.

Stan's Notes: Named for its easily overlooked rosy red belly patch. Mostly a bird of shady woodlands. Excavates holes in rotten wood, looking for spiders, centipedes and beetles. Will hammer acorns and berries into crevices of trees for winter food. Returns to the same tree to excavate a new nest below that of the previous year. Often kicked out of nest hole by European Starlings. Gives a loud "querrr" call and a low "chug-chug-chug." Expanding its range all over the country.

winter pg. 247

breeding

Black-bellied Plover
Pluvialis squatarola

MIGRATION
WINTER

Size: 11-12" (28-30 cm)

Male: Striking black and white breeding plumage. Black belly, chest, sides, face and neck. White cap, nape of neck and belly near tail. Black legs and bill.

Female: less black on belly and chest than male

Juvenile: grayer than adults, with much less black

Nest: ground; male and female construct; 1 brood per year

Eggs: 3-4; pinkish or greenish, marked with blackish brown splotches

Incubation: 26-27 days; male and female incubate, male incubates during the day, female at night

Fledging: 35-45 days; male feeds young, young learn quickly to feed themselves

Migration: complete, to southeastern New Hampshire, southern states, the Gulf Coast, West Indies, Mexico and Central and South America

Food: insects

Compare: A distinctive bird. Look for a black face, chest and belly, and a white cap and nape of neck.

Stan's Notes: Male performs "butterfly" courtship flights to attract females. Female leaves the male and young about 12 days after the eggs hatch. Begins breeding at 3 years of age. A winter resident along coastal New Hampshire and a migrator, seen across New Hampshire and Vermont. During flight, in any plumage, displays a white rump and stripe on the wings with black axillaries (armpits). Often darts across the ground to grab an insect and run.

female pg. 167

male

Bufflehead
Bucephala albeola

MIGRATION
WINTER

Size: 13-15" (33-38 cm)

Male: A small duck with striking white sides and black back. Green purple head with a large white bonnet-like patch.

Female: brown version of male, with a brown head and white patch on cheek, just behind eyes

Juvenile: similar to female

Nest: cavity; female lines an old woodpecker cavity; 1 brood per year

Eggs: 8-10; ivory to olive without markings

Incubation: 29-31 days; female incubates

Fledging: 50-55 days; female leads young to food

Migration: complete, to New Hampshire and Vermont, southern states, Mexico and Central America

Food: aquatic insects

Compare: A small black and white diving duck. Male Hooded Merganser (pg. 65) is similar, but lacks the white sides of male Bufflehead. Look for the green purple head with a large white patch to help identify.

Stan's Notes: This very small, common duck is almost always in small groups or with other ducks. A diving duck, seen on rivers and lakes in New Hampshire and Vermont during migration and winter. Nests in old woodpecker holes. Known to use a burrow in an earthen bank when tree cavities are scarce. Will use a nest box. Uses down feathers to line the nest cavity. Unlike other ducks, the young remain in the nest for up to two days before venturing out with their mothers. Female is very territorial and stays with the same mate for many years.

female pg. 177

male

MIGRATION
WINTER

Lesser Scaup
Aythya affinis

Size: 16-17" (40-43 cm)

Male: Appears mostly black with bold white sides and a gray back. Chest and head look nearly black, but head appears purple with green highlights in direct sun. Bright yellow eyes.

Female: overall brown with a dull white patch at the base of a light gray bill, yellow eyes

Juvenile: same as female

Nest: ground; female builds; 1 brood per year

Eggs: 8-14; olive buff without markings

Incubation: 22-28 days; female incubates

Fledging: 45-50 days; female teaches young to feed

Migration: complete, to southeastern New Hampshire, southern states

Food: aquatic plants and insects

Compare: Male Ring-necked Duck (pg. 63) has a bold white ring on its bill and lacks bold white sides. Male Common Goldeneye (pg. 67) has a white breast. The male Blue-winged Teal (pg. 173) has a white crescent on its bill.

Stan's Notes: A diving duck seen during migration and winter. Often in large flocks numbering in the thousands on lakes, ponds and along the coast. Submerges itself completely to feed on the bottom of lakes (unlike dabbling ducks, which only tip forward to reach the bottom). Note the bold white stripe under the wings when in flight. Male leaves the female when she starts incubating eggs. The quantity of eggs (clutch size) increases with the age of the female. This species has an interesting baby-sitting arrangement in which groups of young (crèches) are tended by 1-3 adult females.

female pg. 179

male

Ring-necked Duck
Aythya collaris

MIGRATION SUMMER

Size: 17" (43 cm)

Male: Striking duck with a black head, breast and back. Sides are gray to nearly white. A light blue bill with a bold white ring and second ring at the base of bill. Top of head is peaked.

Female: dark brown back, light brown sides, a gray face, dark brown crown, white line behind eyes, white ring around a light blue bill, top of head is peaked

Juvenile: similar to female

Nest: ground; female builds; 1 brood per year

Eggs: 8-10; olive gray to brown without markings

Incubation: 26-27 days; female incubates

Fledging: 49-56 days; female teaches young to feed

Migration: complete, to southern states

Food: aquatic plants and insects

Compare: Male Lesser Scaup (pg. 61) has a similar size, but it has a gray back. Look for the bold white ring around the bill of the male Ring-necked Duck.

Stan's Notes: A summer resident and migrator in New Hampshire and Vermont. Usually seen in larger freshwater lakes. A diving duck, watch for it to dive underwater to forage for food. Takes to flight by springing up off the water. Was named "Ring-necked" for its cinnamon-colored collar (nearly impossible to see in the field). Also called Ring-billed Duck due to the white ring on its bill.

female pg. 187

male

YEAR-ROUND
SUMMER

Hooded Merganser
Lophodytes cucullatus

Size:	16-19" (40-48 cm)
Male:	Sleek black-and-white bird with rusty brown sides. Raised crest "hood" shows off a large white patch. A long, thin black bill.
Female:	brown and rust plumage, ragged rusty crest, a long, thin brown bill, yellow-to-gold eyes
Juvenile:	similar to female, brown eyes
Nest:	cavity; female lines an old woodpecker cavity; 1 brood per year
Eggs:	10-12; white without markings
Incubation:	32-33 days; female incubates
Fledging:	71 days; female feeds young
Migration:	complete to partial migrator in New Hampshire and Vermont
Food:	small fish, aquatic insects
Compare:	Male Bufflehead (pg. 59) is smaller and has white sides. Male Wood Duck (pg. 269) is similar in size, but it has a green head. Look for the large white patch on the head and rusty brown sides to help identify the male Hooded Merganser.

Stan's Notes: Small diving bird of shallow ponds, sloughs, lakes and rivers. The male Hoodie voluntarily raises and lowers his crest "hood" to show off his large white head patch. Rarely found away from wooded areas, where it nests in natural cavities or nest boxes. The female will "dump" her eggs in other Hoodie or Wood Duck nests, which results in 20-25 eggs in some nests. Known to share nest cavities with Common Goldeneyes and Wood Ducks, sitting side by side.

female pg. 191

male

Common Goldeneye
Bucephala clangula

MIGRATION
SUMMER
WINTER

Size: 18½-19½" (47-49.5 cm)

Male: A mostly white duck with a black back and large, puffy green head. Large white spot in front of each bright golden eye. Dark bill.

Female: large dark brown head, gray body, white collar, bright golden eyes and yellow-tipped dark bill

Juvenile: same as female, but has a dark bill

Nest: cavity; female lines an old woodpecker cavity; 1 brood per year

Eggs: 8-10; light green without markings

Incubation: 28-32 days; female incubates

Fledging: 56-59 days; female leads young to food

Migration: complete, to southeastern New Hampshire, southern states, Mexico

Food: aquatic plants, insects, fish, mollusks

Compare: Similar to the black and white male Lesser Scaup (pg. 61), which is smaller. Look for a white chest, golden eyes and round white spot in front of each eye to identify the male Common Goldeneye.

Stan's Notes: Known for its loud whistling in flight, produced by its wings. In late winter and early spring, the male often attracts a female through elaborate displays, throwing his head back while uttering a raspy note. Female will lay eggs in other goldeneye nests, resulting in some mothers incubating up to 30 eggs. Received the common name from its obvious bright golden eyes.

male

female

Pileated Woodpecker
Dryocopus pileatus

YEAR-ROUND

Size: 19" (48 cm)

Male: Crow-sized woodpecker with a black back and bright red crest. Long gray bill with red mustache. White leading edge of the wings flashes brightly when flying.

Female: same as male, but has a black forehead and lacks a red mustache

Juvenile: similar to adults, only duller and browner

Nest: cavity; male and female excavate; 1 brood per year

Eggs: 3-5; white without markings

Incubation: 15-18 days; female and male incubate, female incubates during the day, male at night

Fledging: 26-28 days; female and male feed young

Migration: non-migrator

Food: insects; will come to suet feeders

Compare: This bird is quite distinctive and unlikely to be confused with any others. Look for the bright red crest and exceptionally large size of the Pileated.

Stan's Notes: Our largest woodpecker. The common name comes from the Latin *pileatus*, which means "wearing a cap," referring to its crest. A relatively shy bird that prefers large tracts of woodland. Drums on hollow branches, chimneys and so forth to announce its territory. Excavates oval holes up to several feet long in tree trunks, looking for insects to eat. Large wood chips lie at the base of excavated trees. Favorite food is carpenter ants. Feeds young regurgitated insects. Young emerge from the nest looking just like the adults.

Black-crowned Night-Heron
Nycticorax nycticorax

MIGRATION
SUMMER

Size: 22-27" (56-69 cm); up to 3½-foot wingspan

Male: A stocky, hunched, inactive heron with a black back and crown, white belly and gray wings. Long dark bill and bright red eyes. Short yellow legs. Breeding adult has two long white plumes on crown.

Female: same as male

Juvenile: golden brown head and back with white spots, a streaked breast, yellow orange eyes, brown bill

Nest: platform; female and male construct; 1 brood per year

Eggs: 3-5; light blue without markings

Incubation: 24-26 days; female and male incubate

Fledging: 42-48 days; female and male feed young

Migration: complete, to southern states, Mexico and Central America

Food: fish, crabs, crayfish, aquatic insects

Compare: Half the size of Great Blue Heron (pg. 265) when perching. Look for a short-necked heron with a black back and crown.

Stan's Notes: A secretive bird, this heron is most active near dawn and dusk (crepuscular). It hunts alone but nests in small colonies. Roosts in trees during the day. Often squawks when disturbed at the daytime roost. Often harassed by other herons during the day. Stalks quiet backwaters in search of small fish and crabs.

soaring

Osprey
Pandion haliaetus

MIGRATION SUMMER

Size: 21-24" (53-60 cm); up to 5½-foot wingspan

Male: Large eagle-like bird with a white chest and belly and a nearly black back. White head with a black streak through the eyes. Large wings with black "wrist" marks. Dark bill.

Female: same as male, but larger with a necklace of brown streaking

Juvenile: similar to adults, with a light tan breast

Nest: platform, often on a raised wooden platform; female and male build; 1 brood per year

Eggs: 2-4; white with brown markings

Incubation: 32-42 days; female and male incubate

Fledging: 48-58 days; male and female feed young

Migration: complete, to southern states, Florida

Food: fish

Compare: Bald Eagle (pg. 79) is on average 10 inches (25 cm) larger with an all-white head and tail. Juvenile Bald Eagle is brown with white speckles. Look for a white belly and dark stripe through the eyes to identify the Osprey.

Stan's Notes: Ospreys are in a family all their own. It is the only raptor that plunges into water feet first to catch fish. Can hover for a few seconds before diving. Carries fish in a head-first position for better aerodynamics. Often harassed by Bald Eagles for its catch. In flight, wings are angled (cocked) backward. Nests on man-made towers and in tall dead trees. Recent studies show Ospreys mate for a long time, perhaps for life. Northern birds may not migrate to the same wintering grounds. Once almost extinct. Introduced to many regions and now doing well.

juvenile

breeding

Great Black-backed Gull
Larus marinus

YEAR-ROUND
MIGRATION

Size: 30" (76 cm); up to 5½-foot wingspan

Male: An extremely large gull. Black and white breeding plumage with a white head, chest and belly, and black back and wings. Has a distinctive yellow bill with an orange mark near the end of the lower bill. Pink legs.

Female: same as male

Juvenile: gray and brown, lacks any large black spots, has a gray bill

Nest: ground; male and female construct; 1 brood per year

Eggs: 2-3; olive with sparse brown markings

Incubation: 26-29 days; female and male incubate

Fledging: 49-56 days; male and female feed young

Migration: complete, to southern states

Food: fish, insects, crustaceans

Compare: Larger than the Ring-billed Gull (pg. 297) and Herring Gull (pg. 299). Look for a white head, black back and bright yellow bill with an orange spot.

Stan's Notes: One of the largest gulls. A four-year gull, meaning it undergoes four distinct color phases to reach adulthood. Phases are often hard to distinguish and depend upon the amount of black on the bird. First-year gull lacks black on the back and has a gray bill. Second summer gull has small amounts of black and a pale yellow bill with a black tip. Third summer gull has much more black on the back and wings and a black-tipped yellow bill. Fourth summer gull or breeding adult has a black back and wings.

winter

breeding

Common Loon
Gavia immer

MIGRATION
SUMMER
WINTER

Size: 28-36" (71-90 cm)

Male: Breeding adult has a black-and-white back with a checkerboard pattern, a black head, white necklace, deep red eyes and a long, pointed black bill. Winter adult has an all-gray body and bill.

Female: same as male

Juvenile: similar to winter adult, lacks red eyes

Nest: platform, on the ground; female and male build; 1 brood per year

Eggs: 2; olive brown, occasionally brown markings

Incubation: 26-31 days; female and male incubate

Fledging: 75-80 days; female and male feed young

Migration: complete, to southeastern New Hampshire, southern states, the Gulf Coast, Mexico

Food: fish, aquatic insects

Compare: The Double-crested Cormorant (pg. 43) has a black chest and gray bill with yellow at the base and a hooked tip.

Stan's Notes: A true symbol of the wildness of our lakes. Prefers clear lakes because it hunts for fish by eyesight. Legs are set so far back that it has a difficult time walking on land, but it is a great swimmer. The common name comes from the Swedish word *lom*, meaning "lame," for the awkward way it walks on land. Its unique call suggests the wild laughter of a demented person and led to the phrase "crazy as a loon." The young ride on the backs of swimming parents. Adults perform distraction displays to protect young. Very sensitive to disturbance during nesting and will abandon the nest.

soaring

juvenile

soaring
juvenile

YEAR-ROUND
SUMMER
WINTER

Bald Eagle
Haliaeetus leucocephalus

Size: 31-37" (79-94 cm); up to 7½-foot wingspan

Male: Pure white head and tail contrast with a dark brown-to-black body and wings. Large, curved yellow bill and yellow feet.

Female: same as male, only slightly larger

Juvenile: dark brown with white spots or speckles throughout the body and wings, gray bill

Nest: massive platform, usually in a tree; female and male build; 1 brood per year

Eggs: 2-3; off-white without markings

Incubation: 34-36 days; female and male incubate

Fledging: 75-90 days; female and male feed young

Migration: complete, to New Hampshire and Vermont

Food: fish, carrion, birds (mainly ducks)

Compare: The Turkey Vulture (pg. 41) is smaller, has two-toned wings and holds them in a V shape during flight unlike Bald Eagle, which holds its wings straight out.

Stan's Notes: Driven to near extinction due to DDT poisoning and illegal killing. Now making a comeback in North America. Returns to the same nest each year, adding more sticks and enlarging it to massive proportions, at times up to 1,000 pounds (450 kg). In the midair mating ritual, one eagle flips upside down and locks talons with another. Both tumble, then break apart to continue flight. Not uncommon for juvenile eagles to perform this mating ritual even though they have not reached breeding age. Thought to mate for life but will switch mates when not successful at reproducing. Juvenile attains the white head and tail at 4-5 years of age.

SUMMER

Blue-gray Gnatcatcher
Polioptila caerulea

Size: 4" (10 cm)

Male: A light blue-to-gray head, back, breast and wings, with a black forehead and eyebrows. White belly and prominent white eye-ring. Long black tail with a white undertail, often held cocked above the rest of body.

Female: same as male, only grayer and lacking black on the head

Juvenile: similar to female

Nest: cup; female and male build; 1 brood

Eggs: 4-5; pale blue with dark markings

Incubation: 10-13 days; female and male incubate

Fledging: 10-12 days; female and male feed young

Migration: complete, to southern states, the Bahamas, Mexico and Central America

Food: insects

Compare: The only small blue bird with a black tail. Very active near the nest, look for it flitting around upper branches in search of insects.

Stan's Notes: Can be seen in a wide variety of forest types in New Hampshire and Vermont during summer. Listen for its wheezy call notes to help locate. A fun and easy bird to watch. Flicks its tail up and down and from side to side while calling. Like many open woodland nesters, it is a common cowbird host. In many years, it nests so early that by mid-June it is no longer defending territory. Although the population is abundant, it has been decreasing in the recent past.

female pg. 115

male

Indigo Bunting
Passerina cyanea

SUMMER

Size:	5½" (14 cm)
Male:	Vibrant blue finch-like bird. Scattered dark markings on wings and tail.
Female:	light brown bird with faint markings
Juvenile:	similar to female
Nest:	cup; female builds; 2 broods per year
Eggs:	3-4; pale blue without markings
Incubation:	12-13 days; female incubates
Fledging:	10-11 days; female feeds young
Migration:	complete, to Florida, Mexico and Central and South America
Food:	insects, seeds, fruit; will visit seed feeders
Compare:	Male Eastern Bluebird (pg. 89) is larger and has a rusty red breast.

Stan's Notes: Usually only the males are noticed. Actually a gray bird, without any blue pigment in its feathers. As seen in Blue Jays and other blue birds, sunlight is refracted within the structure of the male bunting's feathers, making them look blue. Appears to be iridescent in direct sunlight. Molts to acquire body feathers with gray tips, which quickly wear off, revealing bright blue plumage in spring. Molts again in fall and appears like the females during winter. Males often sing from treetops to attract mates. Will come to seed feeders in spring before insects are plentiful. Mostly seen along woodland edges, feeding on insects. Migrates at night in flocks of 5-10 birds. Males return before the females and juveniles, usually to the previous year's nest site. Juveniles move to within a mile from their birth site.

Tree Swallow
Tachycineta bicolor

Size: 5-6" (13-15 cm)

Male: Blue green during spring and greener in fall. Appears to change color in direct sunlight. White chin, breast and belly. Long, pointed wing tips. Notched tail.

Female: similar to male, only duller

Juvenile: gray brown with a white belly and grayish breast band

Nest: cavity; female and male line old woodpecker cavity or nest box; 2 broods per year

Eggs: 4-6; white without markings

Incubation: 13-16 days; female incubates

Fledging: 20-24 days; female and male feed young

Migration: complete, to southern states, Mexico and Central America

Food: insects

Compare: Similar color as the Purple Martin (pg. 91), but smaller with a white breast and belly. The Barn Swallow (pg. 87) has a rust belly and deeply forked tail.

Stan's Notes: Most common at ponds, lakes and agricultural fields during summer. Can be attracted to your yard with a nest box. Competes with Eastern Bluebirds for cavities and nest boxes. Will travel great distances to find dropped feathers to line its grass nest. Occasionally seen playing, chasing after dropped feathers. Often seen flying back and forth across fields, feeding on insects. A good bird to have around because it eats many nuisance insects. Gathers in large flocks during migration.

Barn Swallow
Hirundo rustica

SUMMER

Size: 7" (18 cm)

Male: A sleek swallow. Blue black back, cinnamon belly and reddish brown chin. White spots on a long, deeply forked tail.

Female: same as male, but has a whiter chest

Juvenile: similar to adults, with a tan belly and chin and a shorter tail

Nest: cup; female and male construct; 2 broods per year

Eggs: 4-5; white with brown markings

Incubation: 13-17 days; female incubates

Fledging: 18-23 days; female and male feed young

Migration: complete, to South America

Food: insects, prefers beetles, wasps and flies

Compare: Tree Swallow (pg. 85) has a white belly and chin, and a notched tail. The Chimney Swift (pg. 101) has wings that are longer than the length of its body, and a narrow pointed tail. The Purple Martin (pg. 91) is nearly 2 inches (5 cm) larger and has a dark purple belly.

Stan's Notes: Of the six swallow species in New Hampshire and Vermont, this is the only one that has a deeply forked tail. Unlike other swallows, Barn Swallows rarely glide in flight, so look for continuous flapping. Builds a mud nest using up to 1,000 beak-loads of mud, often on barns, houses, under bridges or nearly any place that provides some shelter. Nests in colonies of 4-6 birds, but nesting alone is not uncommon. Drinks in flight, skimming water or getting water from wet leaves. Also bathes while flying through rain or sprinklers.

Eastern Bluebird
Sialia sialis

SUMMER

Size: 7" (18 cm)

Male: Reminiscent of its larger cousin, the American Robin, with a rusty red breast and a white belly. Sky blue head, back and tail.

Female: shares the rusty red breast and white belly, but grayer with a faint blue tail and wings

Juvenile: similar to female, with spots on chest, blue wing markings

Nest: cavity, old woodpecker cavity or man-made nest box; female builds; 2 broods per year

Eggs: 4-5; pale blue without markings

Incubation: 12-14 days; female incubates

Fledging: 15-18 days; male and female feed young

Migration: complete, to southern states

Food: insects, fruit

Compare: The male Indigo Bunting (pg. 83) is nearly all blue, lacking the rusty red breast. Blue Jay (pg. 93) is much larger and has a crest.

Stan's Notes: Summer bird of open fields and agricultural areas. Once nearly eliminated from New Hampshire and Vermont due to the lack of nest cavities, bluebirds have made a remarkable comeback with the aid of bird enthusiasts who have put up thousands of bluebird nest boxes. Easily tamed. Will come to a shallow dish of mealworms. Bluebirds like open habitats such as fields, pastures and roadsides. Will perch in trees or on fence posts and wait for grasshoppers. Sings a distinctive "chur-lee chur chur-lee." Young of the first brood help raise young of the second.

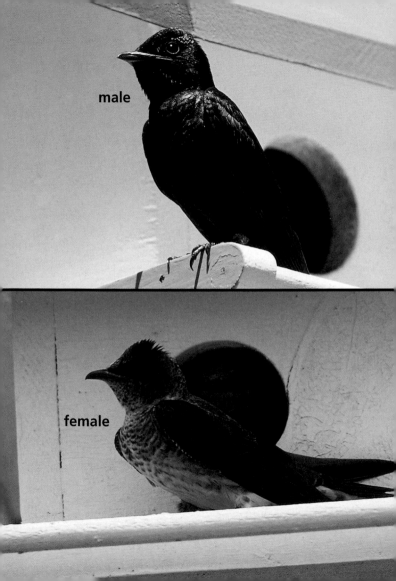

Purple Martin
Progne subis

SUMMER

Size: 8½" (22 cm)

Male: A large swallow-shaped bird with a purple head, back and belly. Black wings and tail. Notched tail.

Female: gray purple head and back with a whitish belly, darker wings and tail

Juvenile: same as female

Nest: cavity; female and male line the cavity of the house; 1 brood per year

Eggs: 4-5; white without markings

Incubation: 15-18 days; female incubates

Fledging: 26-30 days; male and female feed young

Migration: complete, to South America

Food: insects

Compare: The male is the only swallow with a dark purple belly. Usually seen only in groups.

Stan's Notes: The largest swallow species in North America. Once nested in tree cavities, but now nearly exclusively nests in man-made nest boxes in New Hampshire and Vermont. Main diet consists of dragonflies, not mosquitoes as was once thought. Often drinks and bathes during flight by skimming water or flying through rain. Will return to the same nest site each year. Males arrive before females and yearlings. Frequently nests within 100 feet (30 m) of a human dwelling and, in fact, the most successful colonies are located within this distance. Young strike out to form new colonies. Huge colonies gather in autumn to migrate to South America.

Blue Jay
Cyanocitta cristata

YEAR-ROUND

Size: 12" (30 cm)

Male: Large, bright light blue and white bird with a black necklace. Crest moves up and down at will. White face with a gray belly. White wing bars on blue wings. Black spots and a white tip on blue tail.

Female: same as male

Juvenile: same as adult, only duller

Nest: cup; female and male construct; 1-2 broods per year

Eggs: 4-5; green to blue with brown markings

Incubation: 16-18 days; female incubates

Fledging: 17-21 days; female and male feed young

Migration: non-migrator to partial; will move around in winter to find an abundant food source

Food: insects, fruit, carrion, seeds, nuts; comes to seed feeders, also ground feeders with corn

Compare: The Eastern Bluebird (pg. 89) is much smaller and lacks the Jay's white markings and crest. Belted Kingfisher (pg. 95) lacks the vivid blue coloring and black necklace of the Jay.

Stan's Notes: Highly intelligent bird, solving problems, gathering food and communicating more than the other birds. Screams like a hawk to scatter birds at feeders. Known as the alarm of the forest, screaming at intruders in the woods. Eats bird eggs and young birds in other nests. One of the few birds to cache food. Feathers do not have blue pigment; refracted sunlight casts the blue light. In flight, carries seeds and nuts in a pouch under its tongue (sublingual) to the nest for its young, or elsewhere to eat the food in safety.

Belted Kingfisher
Megaceryle alcyon

YEAR-ROUND SUMMER

Size: 13" (33 cm)

Male: Large blue bird with a white belly. Broad blue gray breast band and a ragged crest that is raised and lowered at will. Large head with a long, thick black bill. A small white spot directly in front of red brown eyes. Black wing tips with splashes of white that flash when flying.

Female: same as male, but with a rusty breast band in addition to blue gray band, and rusty flanks

Juvenile: similar to female

Nest: cavity; female and male excavate; 1 brood per year

Eggs: 6-7; white without markings

Incubation: 23-24 days; female and male incubate

Fledging: 23-24 days; female and male feed young

Migration: non-migrator to partial in New Hampshire and Vermont; will move around in winter to find food

Food: small fish

Compare: Kingfisher is darker blue than the Blue Jay (pg. 93) and has a larger, more ragged crest. Kingfisher is rarely found away from water.

Stan's Notes: Perched on a branch near water, it will dive head-first for small fish and return to the branch to feed. Gives a loud machine-gun-like call. Digs a deep nest cavity in the bank of a river or lake. Parents drop dead fish into water, teaching the young to dive. Can't pass bones through its digestive tract; regurgitates bone pellets after meals. Mates recognize each other by call.

Chestnut-sided Warbler
Setophaga pensylvanica

SUMMER

Size: 5" (13 cm)

Male: A colorful combination of a yellow cap and black mask set against a white face, chin, breast and belly. Two yellow wing bars on gray wings. Chestnut flanks.

Female: similar to male, flanks are duller brown

Juvenile: similar to female, but has a lime green head and back, white eye-ring, bright yellow wing bars, lacks chestnut sides

Nest: cup; female builds; 1 brood per year

Eggs: 3-5; white with brown markings

Incubation: 12-13 days; female incubates

Fledging: 10-12 days; female and male feed young

Migration: complete, to Central America

Food: insects, berries

Compare: Shares the yellow cap with Yellow-rumped Warbler (pg. 225), but lacks the yellow sides and rump. The Yellow Warbler (pg. 313) is nearly all yellow and lacks the white breast and chestnut flanks of the Chestnut-sided.

Stan's Notes: The common name for this attractive warbler comes from the chestnut patches on its sides. During migration, it is often attracted to backyard water gardens with small trickling streams. Prefers an open, young aspen forest. Look for it in spring, hopping high up in branches while it hunts for insects. You will usually only get a glimpse of it because it is a fast-moving bird. Holds its tail in an uplifted position, showing the white undertail. Not uncommon for it to approach humans in defense of a nest site.

Brown Creeper
Certhia americana

YEAR-ROUND

Size: 5" (13 cm)

Male: Small, thin, nearly camouflaged brown bird. White from chin to belly. White eyebrows. Long stiff tail. Dark eyes. Thin curved bill.

Female: same as male

Juvenile: same as adult

Nest: cup; female constructs; unknown number of broods per year

Eggs: 5-6; white with tiny brown markings

Incubation: 14-17 days; female incubates, male feeds the female during incubation

Fledging: 13-16 days; female and male feed young

Migration: partial to non-migrator

Food: insects, nuts, seeds

Compare: Creeps up tree trunks, not down, like the White-breasted Nuthatch (pg. 223). Watch for Brown Creeper to fly from the top of one trunk to the bottom of another, then work its way to the top, looking for insects. Slightly larger than Red-breasted Nuthatch (pg. 219), with a similar white stripe above the eyes, but Brown Creeper has a white belly, long tail and lacks a black cap.

Stan's Notes: This bird utilizes its camouflage coloring to defend itself, spreading out flat on a branch or tree trunk without moving. Young are able to follow their parents, creeping soon after fledging. Commonly found in wooded areas. Often builds nest behind loose bark of dead or dying trees.

Chimney Swift
Chaetura pelagica

SUMMER

Size: 5" (13 cm)

Male: Nondescript, swallow-shaped bird, usually seen only in flight. A long, thin brown body with a pointed tail and head. Long swept-back wings, longer than the body.

Female: same as male

Juvenile: same as adult

Nest: half cup; female and male construct; 1 brood per year

Eggs: 4-5; white without markings

Incubation: 19-21 days; female and male incubate

Fledging: 28-30 days; female and male feed young

Migration: complete, to South America

Food: insects caught in air

Compare: Considerably smaller than the Purple Martin (pg. 91) and lacks the iridescent purple. Barn Swallow (pg. 87) has a forked tail unlike the Swift's pointed tail. Tree Swallow (pg. 85) has a white belly and blue green back.

Stan's Notes: One of the fastest fliers in the bird world. Spends all day flying, rarely perching. Bathes and drinks by skimming across water surfaces. Unique in-flight twittering call is often heard before the bird is seen. Flies in groups, feeding on flying insects 100 feet (30 m) or higher in the air. Often called Flying Cigar due to its pointed body shape. Hundreds roost in large chimneys, hence the common name. Builds nest with tiny twigs, cementing it with saliva, attaching it to the inside of a chimney or hollow tree. Usually only one nest per chimney.

SUMMER

Chipping Sparrow
Spizella passerina

Size: 5" (13 cm)

Male: Small gray brown sparrow with a clear gray breast, rusty crown and white eyebrows. A black eye line and thin gray black bill. Two faint wing bars.

Female: same as male

Juvenile: similar to adult, has a streaked breast, lacks the rusty crown

Nest: cup; female builds; 2 broods per year

Eggs: 3-5; blue green with brown markings

Incubation: 11-14 days; female incubates

Fledging: 10-12 days; female and male feed young

Migration: complete, to southern states, Mexico and Central America

Food: insects, seeds; will come to ground feeders

Compare: Song Sparrow (pg. 119) is larger and has a heavily streaked breast. The American Tree Sparrow (pg. 121) shares a rusty crown, but lacks the black eye line. The Fox Sparrow (pg. 131) lacks a plain chest. Female House Finch (pg. 109) has a streaked chest.

Stan's Notes: A common garden or yard bird, often seen feeding on dropped seeds beneath feeders. Gathers in large family groups to feed in preparation for migration. Migrates at night in flocks of 20-30 birds. The common name comes from the male's fast "chip" call. Often just called Chippy. Builds nest low in dense shrubs and almost always lines it with animal hair. Can be very unafraid of people, allowing you to approach closely before it flies away.

male

female

Common Redpoll
Acanthis flammea

Size: 5" (13 cm)

Male: A small sparrow-like bird with a bright red crown and black spot on the chin. Heavily streaked back and a splash of raspberry red on the chest.

Female: same as male, but lacking raspberry red on the chest

Juvenile: browner than adults, lacks a red crown, has dark streaks on the chest

Nest: cup; female builds; 1 brood (occasionally 2) per year

Eggs: 4-5; pale green with purple markings

Incubation: 10-11 days; female incubates

Fledging: 11-12 days; female and male feed young

Migration: irruptive; moves into New Hampshire and Vermont from Canada in some winters

Food: seeds, insects; will come to seed feeders

Compare: Same size as Pine Siskin (pg. 107), which has yellow wing bars and lacks the red crown. Look for the bright red crown and black spot under the bill.

Stan's Notes: Winters in New Hampshire and Vermont after summering in the far reaches of Canada. Comes to seed feeders in small to large flocks. Winter flocks of as many as 100 birds are not uncommon; not seen at all in some winters. Bathes in snow or open water during winter. Much like Black-capped Chickadees, it can be tamed and hand fed.

Pine Siskin
Spinus pinus

YEAR-ROUND
WINTER

Size: 5" (13 cm)

Male: Small brown finch. A heavily streaked back, breast and belly. Yellow wing bars. Yellow at base of tail. Thin bill.

Female: same as male

Juvenile: similar to adult, light yellow tinge over the breast and chin

Nest: modified cup; female builds; 2 broods

Eggs: 3-4; greenish blue with brown markings

Incubation: 12-13 days; female incubates

Fledging: 14-15 days; female and male feed young

Migration: non-migrator to irruptive; moves around the U.S. in search of food

Food: seeds, insects; will come to seed feeders

Compare: Female American Goldfinch (pg. 307) lacks streaks and has white wing bars. Female House Finch (pg. 109) has a streaked chest, but lacks yellow wing bars. Female Purple Finch (pg. 125) has bold white eyebrows.

Stan's Notes: Often considered a winter finch, it is also a breeding resident in parts of New Hampshire and Vermont. Conspicuous in some winters, absent in others. Seen in flocks of up to 20 birds, often with other species of finches. Gathers in flocks and moves around, visiting feeders. Comes to thistle feeders. Breeds in small groups. Male feeds the female during incubation. Juveniles lose the yellow tint by late summer of their first year. Builds nest toward the end of coniferous branches, where needles are dense, helping to conceal. Nests are often only a few feet apart.

male
pg. 285

female

House Finch
Haemorhous mexicanus

Size: 5" (13 cm)

Female: similar to male, with less yellow

Male: orange red face, chest and rump, brown cap, brown marking behind eyes, brown wings streaked with white, a streaked belly

Juvenile: similar to female

Nest: cup, occasionally in a cavity, female builds; 2 broods per year

Eggs: 4-5; pale blue, lightly marked

Incubation: 12-14 days; female incubates

Fledging: 15-19 days; female and male feed young

Migration: non-migrator to partial; will move around to find food

Food: seeds, fruit, leaf buds; will visit seed feeders

Compare: The female Purple Finch (pg. 125) is very similar, but it has bold white eyebrows. The female American Goldfinch (pg. 307) has a clear chest and white wing bars. Similar to Pine Siskin (pg. 107), but lacks yellow wing bars and has a much larger bill than Siskin.

Stan's Notes: Very social, visiting feeders in small flocks. Can be the most common bird at feeders. Likes to nest in hanging flower baskets. Male sings a loud, cheerful warbling song. House Finches that were originally introduced to Long Island, New York, from the western U.S. in the 1940s have since populated the eastern U.S. Although relatively new to New Hampshire and Vermont, they are now found across the country. Male feeds the incubating female. Suffers from a fatal eye disease that causes the eyes to crust.

House Wren
Troglodytes aedon

SUMMER

Size: 5" (13 cm)

Male: A small all-brown bird with lighter brown markings on tail and wings. Slightly curved brown bill. Often holds its tail erect.

Female: same as male

Juvenile: same as adult

Nest: cavity; female and male line just about any nest cavity; 2 broods per year

Eggs: 4-6; tan with brown markings

Incubation: 10-13 days; female and male incubate

Fledging: 12-15 days; female and male feed young

Migration: complete, to southern states and Mexico

Food: insects, spiders, snails

Compare: House Wren is distinguished from Carolina Wren (pg. 113) by the lack of eyebrows. The long curved bill and long upturned tail differentiates House Wren from sparrows.

Stan's Notes: A prolific songster, it will sing from dawn until dusk during the mating season. Easily attracted to nest boxes. In spring, the male chooses several prospective nesting cavities and places a few small twigs in each. Female inspects each, chooses one, and finishes the nest building. She will completely fill the nest cavity with uniformly small twigs, then line a small depression at the back of the cavity with pine needles and grass. Often has trouble fitting long twigs through the nest cavity hole. Tries many different directions and approaches until successful.

YEAR-ROUND

Carolina Wren
Thryothorus ludovicianus

Size: 5½" (14 cm)

Male: Warm rusty brown head and back with an orange yellow chest and belly. White throat and a prominent white eye stripe. A short stubby tail, often cocked up.

Female: same as male

Juvenile: same as adult

Nest: cavity; female and male build; 2 broods per year, sometimes 3

Eggs: 4-6; white, sometimes pink or creamy, with brown markings

Incubation: 12-14 days; female incubates

Fledging: 12-14 days; female and male feed young

Migration: non-migrator; moves around to find food

Food: insects, fruit, few seeds; visits suet feeders

Compare: Similar to the House Wren (pg. 111), but Carolina Wren is lighter brown and has a prominent white eye stripe.

Stan's Notes: Mates are long-term, staying together throughout the year in permanent territories. Sings year-round. Male is known to sing up to 40 different song types, singing one song repeatedly before switching to another. Female also sings, resulting in duets. The male often takes over feeding the first brood while the female renests. Nests in birdhouses and in unusual places like mailboxes, bumpers or broken taillights of vehicles, or nearly any other cavity. Found in brushy yards or woodlands. Can be attracted to feeders with mealworms.

female

male
pg. 83

Indigo Bunting
Passerina cyanea

SUMMER

Size: 5½" (14 cm)

Female: A light brown finch-like bird. Faint streaking on a light tan chest. Wings have a very faint blue cast with indistinct wing bars.

Male: vibrant blue finch-like bird, scattered dark markings on wings and tail

Juvenile: similar to female

Nest: cup; female builds; 2 broods per year

Eggs: 3-4; pale blue without markings

Incubation: 12-13 days; female incubates

Fledging: 10-11 days; female feeds young

Migration: complete, to Florida, Mexico and Central and South America

Food: insects, seeds, fruit; will visit seed feeders

Compare: Female Purple Finch (pg. 125) has white eyebrows and a heavily streaked chest. Female House Finch (pg. 109) has a heavily streaked chest. Female American Goldfinch (pg. 307) has white wing bars.

Stan's Notes: A secretive bird; usually only the males are noticed. Males often sing from treetops to attract mates. Will come to seed feeders in spring before insects are plentiful. Mostly seen along woodland edges, feeding on insects. Migrates at night in flocks of 5-10 birds. Males return before the females and juveniles, usually to the previous year's nest site. Juveniles move to within a mile from their birth site.

male pg. 227

female

Dark-eyed Junco
Junco hyemalis

YEAR-ROUND

Size: 5½" (14 cm)

Female: Round, dark-eyed bird with a tan-to-brown chest, head and back. White belly. Ivory-to-pink bill. Since the outermost tail feathers are white, tail appears as a white V in flight.

Male: same as female, only slate gray to charcoal

Juvenile: similar to female, but has a streaked breast and head

Nest: cup; female and male construct; 2 broods per year

Eggs: 3-5; white with reddish brown markings

Incubation: 12-13 days; female incubates

Fledging: 10-13 days; male and female feed young

Migration: complete, across the U.S., non-migrator in New Hampshire and Vermont

Food: seeds, insects; will come to seed feeders

Compare: Rarely confused with any other bird. Small flocks feed under bird feeders in winter.

Stan's Notes: A year-round bird in New Hampshire and Vermont, but usually more commonly seen during winter. Adheres to a rigid social hierarchy, with dominant birds chasing less dominant birds. Look for its white outer tail feathers flashing when in flight. Often seen in small flocks on the ground, where it will "double-scratch" with both feet simultaneously to expose seeds and insects. Eats many weed seeds. Constructs its nest in a wide variety of wooded habitats. Several junco species have now been combined into one, simply called Dark-eyed Junco.

Song Sparrow
Melospiza melodia

Size: 5-6" (13-15 cm)

Male: A common brown sparrow with heavy dark streaks on the breast coalescing into a central dark spot.

Female: same as male

Juvenile: similar to adult, finely streaked breast, lacks a central spot

Nest: cup; female builds; 2 broods per year

Eggs: 3-4; pale blue to green, marked with reddish brown splotches

Incubation: 12-14 days; female incubates

Fledging: 9-12 days; female and male feed young

Migration: non-migrator in New Hampshire, Vermont

Food: insects, seeds; rarely visits seed feeders

Compare: Similar to other brown sparrows. Look for the heavily streaked breast with a central dark spot to help identify the Song Sparrow.

Stan's Notes: Many subspecies or varieties of Song Sparrow, but the dark central spot is seen in each variant. Defends a small territory by singing from thick shrubs. This is a constant songster that repeats its loud, clear song every couple minutes. Song varies in structure, but it is basically the same from region to region. A ground feeder, look for it to scratch at the same time with both feet, or "double-scratch," to expose seeds. While the female builds another nest for a second brood, the male often takes over feeding the young. Unlike many other sparrow species, Song Sparrows will rarely flock together. A common host of the Brown-headed Cowbird.

WINTER

American Tree Sparrow
Spizelloides arborea

Size: 6" (15 cm)

Male: A common brown sparrow with a tan breast and rusty crown. Black spot in the center of breast. Upper bill is dark, lower bill yellow. Two white wing bars. Gray eyebrows.

Female: same as male

Juvenile: lacks a rust crown, has a streaked chest that often obscures the central dark spot

Nest: cup; female builds; 1 brood per year

Eggs: 3-5; green white with brown markings

Incubation: 12-13 days; female incubates

Fledging: 8-10 days; female and male feed young

Migration: complete, to New Hampshire, Vermont and throughout North America

Food: insects, seeds; visits seed feeders

Compare: Appears similar to other sparrows, so look at the center of the breast for a single dark spot. Shares the rusty crown with Chipping Sparrow (pg. 103), but lacks the white eyebrows and black eye line. The Song Sparrow (pg. 119) has a heavily streaked chest.

Stan's Notes: A bird feeder visitor throughout New Hampshire and Vermont during winter. Also seen during migration in flocks of 2-200 birds. Sometimes called Winter Chippy because it looks like the Chipping Sparrow. Nests in northern Canada and Alaska. The species name *arborea* means "tree," but it does not nest in trees; common name "Tree" refers to its habitat. Nests on the ground in a clump or tuft of grass. "American" refers to its natural range.

House Sparrow
Passer domesticus

Size: 6" (15 cm)

Male: Medium sparrow-like bird. Large black spot on the throat extending down to the breast. Brown back. One white wing bar. Gray belly and crown.

Female: slightly smaller than the male, light brown, lacks the throat patch and the wing bar

Juvenile: similar to female

Nest: cavity, with a domed cup nest inside; female and male build; 2-3 broods per year

Eggs: 4-6; white with brown markings

Incubation: 10-12 days; female incubates

Fledging: 14-17 days; female and male feed young

Migration: non-migrator; moves around to find food

Food: seeds, insects, fruit; comes to seed feeders

Compare: Lacks the rusty crown of the American Tree Sparrow (pg. 121) and the Chipping Sparrow (pg. 103). Look for the black bib of the male House Sparrow. Female House Sparrow has a clear breast and lacks a rusty crown.

Stan's Notes: One of the first bird songs heard in cities in spring. A familiar city bird, nearly always in small flocks. Also found on farms. Introduced from Europe to Central Park, New York, in 1850, it is now found throughout North America. Related to Old World sparrows; not related to any sparrows in the United States. Builds an oversized domed nest with dried grass, scraps of plastic, paper and whatever else is available. An aggressive bird that will kill the young of other birds in order to take over a cavity.

male
pg. 287

female

YEAR-ROUND

Purple Finch
Haemorhous purpureus

Size: 6" (15 cm)

Female: A plain brown bird with a heavily streaked chest. Prominent white eyebrows.

Male: raspberry red head, cap, breast, back and rump, brownish wings and tail

Juvenile: same as female

Nest: cup; female and male build; 1 brood per year

Eggs: 4-5; greenish blue with brown markings

Incubation: 12-13 days; female incubates

Fledging: 13-14 days; female and male feed young

Migration: non-migrator to partial in New Hampshire and Vermont; moves around during winter to find food

Food: seeds, insects, fruit; comes to seed feeders

Compare: Female House Finch (pg. 109) lacks female Purple Finch's white eyebrows. Pine Siskin (pg. 107) has yellow wing bars and a much smaller bill than Purple Finch. The female American Goldfinch (pg. 307) has a clear chest and white wing bars.

Stan's Notes: A year-round resident throughout New Hampshire and Vermont, and New Hampshire's state bird. Travels in flocks of up to 50 individuals. Visits seed feeders along with House Finches, making it hard to tell them apart. Feeds mainly on seeds, with ash tree seeds an important source of food. Prefers open woods or woodland edges. Sings a rich, loud song, giving a distinctive "tic" note only in flight. Not a purple color, the Latin species name *purpureus* means "crimson" or other reddish color.

White-throated Sparrow
Zonotrichia albicollis

YEAR-ROUND SUMMER

Size: 6-7" (15-18 cm)

Male: Brown bird with a gray tan chest and belly. A small yellow spot between the eyes (lore). Distinctive white or tan throat patch. White or tan stripes alternate with black stripes on crown. Color of the throat patch and crown stripes match.

Female: same as male

Juvenile: similar to adult, gray throat and eyebrows with a heavily streaked chest

Nest: cup; female builds; 1 brood per year

Eggs: 4-6; color varies from greenish to bluish to creamy white with red brown markings

Incubation: 11-14 days; female incubates

Fledging: 10-12 days; female and male feed young

Migration: complete, to southern states and Mexico

Food: insects, seeds, fruit; visits ground feeders

Compare: White-crowned Sparrow (pg. 129) lacks a throat patch and yellow lore.

Stan's Notes: Two color variations (polymorphic): white-striped and tan-striped. Studies indicate that the white-striped adults tend to mate with the tan-striped birds. No indication why. Known for its wonderful song. Sings all year and can even be heard at night. White- and tan-striped males and white-striped females sing, but tan-striped females do not. Builds nest on the ground under small trees in bogs and coniferous forests. Often associated with other sparrows in winter. Feeds on the ground under feeders. Immature and first-year females tend to winter farther south than adults.

127

juvenile

White-crowned Sparrow
Zonotrichia leucophrys

Size: 6½-7½" (16-19 cm)

Male: A brown sparrow with a gray breast and a black-and-white striped crown. Small, thin pink bill.

Female: same as male

Juvenile: similar to adult, with brown stripes on the head instead of white

Nest: cup; female builds; 2 broods per year

Eggs: 3-5; color varies from greenish to bluish to whitish with red brown markings

Incubation: 11-14 days; female incubates

Fledging: 8-12 days; male and female feed young

Migration: complete, to southern states and Mexico

Food: insects, seeds, berries; visits ground feeders

Compare: The White-throated Sparrow (pg. 127) has a white or tan throat patch and blackish bill, with a small yellow spot between the eyes and bill. Song Sparrow (pg. 119) has heavy dark streaks on the breast coalescing into a central spot.

Stan's Notes: A prolific songster. Usually in groups of as many as 20 birds during migration, when it can be seen feeding underneath seed feeders. Males arrive on the breeding grounds before females and establish territories by singing from perches. A ground feeder, scratching backward with both feet at the same time. Male takes most of the responsibility to raise the young while female starts the second brood. Only 9-12 days separate broods. Nests in Canada and Alaska.

Fox Sparrow
Passerella iliaca

MIGRATION

Size: 7" (18 cm)

Male: A plump, rusty red sparrow with a heavily streaked, rust-colored breast and solid rust tail. Head and back are mottled with gray.

Female: same as male

Juvenile: same as adult

Nest: cup; female builds; 2 broods per year

Eggs: 2-4; pale green with reddish markings

Incubation: 12-14 days; female incubates

Fledging: 10-11 days; female and male feed young

Migration: complete, to southern states

Food: insects, seeds; comes to feeders

Compare: Similar coloration as the Brown Thrasher (pg. 159), but the Fox Sparrow is smaller, plumper and has a smaller bill. Rusty color differentiates it from all other sparrows.

Stan's Notes: One of the largest sparrows. Several color variations, depending upon the part of the country. Usually seen only under seed feeders during migration and winter, searching for seeds and insects. Scratches like a chicken with both feet at the same time to find food. Usually alone or in small groups. The common name "Sparrow" comes from the Anglo-Saxon word *spearwa*, meaning "flutterer," as applied to any small bird. "Fox" refers to its rusty color. Nests on the ground in brush and along forest edges in Canada and Alaska.

Hermit Thrush
Catharus guttatus

SUMMER

Size: 7" (18 cm)

Male: Brown head, nape of neck and back with a heavily streaked or spotted white chest. Tail and edge of wings are rusty red. Thin white ring around each eye. Short thin bill. Often holds wings in a dropped position with tail cocked slightly upward.

Female: same as male

Juvenile: similar to adult

Nest: cup; female builds; 1-2 broods per year

Eggs: 3-6; greenish blue without markings

Incubation: 12-14 days; female incubates

Fledging: 12-14 days; female and male feed young

Migration: complete, to southern states

Food: insects, fruit, spiders, earthworms

Compare: Smaller than the Wood Thrush (pg. 145), which lacks the rusty red tail and edge of wings. Much smaller than Brown Thrasher (pg. 159), which has a longer curving bill and bright yellow eyes.

Stan's Notes: This is the state bird of Vermont. A highly migratory thrush that prefers mixed forest habitat and forest edges. Feeds mainly on the ground, similar to American Robins. Runs forward, stops and cocks its head, looking for movement. Often stands with its wings dropped down and rusty red tail cocked upward. Frequently raises and lowers its tail, giving a soft clucking note after landing on a perch. Habitually flicks its wings when perched.

Horned Lark
Eremophila alpestris

YEAR-ROUND

Size: 7-8" (18-20 cm)

Male: A sleek tan-to-brown bird. Black necklace with a yellow chin and black bill. Two tiny "horns" on the top of head; can be difficult to see. A dark tail with white outer feathers, noticeable in flight.

Female: duller than male, "horns" less noticeable

Juvenile: lacks the black markings and yellow chin, doesn't form "horns" until second year

Nest: ground; female builds; 2-3 broods per year

Eggs: 3-4; gray with brown markings

Incubation: 11-12 days; female incubates

Fledging: 9-12 days; female and male feed young

Migration: non-migrator to partial in New Hampshire and Vermont

Food: seeds, insects

Compare: Smaller than Meadowlark (pg. 333), which shares the black necklace and yellow chin. Look for black marks in front of the eyes.

Stan's Notes: The only true lark native to North America. Moves around during winter to find food. Horned Larks are birds of open ground. Common in rural areas, frequently seen in large flocks. Population increased in North America over the past century due to the clearing of land for farming. Can have up to three broods per year because the birds get such an early start. Male performs a fluttering courtship flight high in the air while singing a high-pitched song. Female performs a fluttering distraction display if the nest is disturbed. Can renest about a week after the brood fledges. "Lark" comes from the Middle English word *laverock*, or "a lark."

female

male
pg. 49

SUMMER

Rose-breasted Grosbeak
Pheucticus ludovicianus

Size: 7-8" (18-20 cm)

Female: A plump, heavily streaked brown and white bird with obvious white eyebrows. Orange yellow wing linings.

Male: black-and-white bird with a large, triangular rose patch in the center of chest, wing linings are rosy red

Juvenile: similar to female

Nest: cup; female and male construct; 1-2 broods per year

Eggs: 3-5; blue green with brown markings

Incubation: 13-14 days; female and male incubate

Fledging: 9-12 days; female and male feed young

Migration: complete, to Mexico, Central America and South America

Food: insects, seeds, fruit; comes to seed feeders

Compare: Looks like a large sparrow. Larger and has a more distinctive eyebrow mark than female Purple Finch (pg. 125). The female House Finch (pg. 109) lacks the eyebrow mark.

Stan's Notes: Usually prefers a mature deciduous forest for nesting. Both sexes sing, but the male sings much louder and clearer. Has a rich, robin-like song. Common name "Grosbeak" refers to its large bill, used to crush seeds. Seen during spring and migration. Males arrive at their destinations first, joined by females several days later. Several will come to seed feeders at the same time in spring. When females arrive, males become territorial and reduce visits to feeders. Young grosbeaks visit feeders with the adults after fledging.

female

male
pg. 25

Eastern Towhee
Pipilo erythrophthalmus

Size: 7-8" (18-20 cm)

Female: A mostly light brown bird. Rusty red brown sides and white belly. Long brown tail with a white tip. Short, stout, pointed bill and rich red eyes. White wing patches flash in flight.

Male: similar to female, but is black, not brown

Juvenile: light brown with heavily streaked head, chest and belly, long dark tail with a white tip

Nest: cup; female builds; 2 broods per year

Eggs: 3-4; creamy white with brown markings

Incubation: 12-13 days; female incubates

Fledging: 10-12 days; male and female feed young

Migration: complete, to southern states, South America

Food: insects, seeds, fruit; visits ground feeders

Compare: Slightly smaller than the American Robin (pg. 243), which has a red breast and lacks the white belly. Female Rose-breasted Grosbeak (pg. 137) has a heavily streaked breast and obvious white eyebrows.

Stan's Notes: Common name comes from its distinctive "tow-hee" call given by both sexes. Mostly known for its characteristic call that sounds like, "Drink-your-tea!" Seen hopping backward with both feet (bilateral scratching), raking up leaf litter for insects and seeds. The female broods, but the male does most of the feeding of young. In southern coastal states, some have red eyes; others have white eyes. The red-eyed variety is seen in New Hampshire and Vermont.

male pg. 27

female

Brown-headed Cowbird
Molothrus ater

YEAR-ROUND
SUMMER

Size: 7½" (19 cm)

Female: Dull brown bird with no obvious markings. Pointed, sharp gray bill. Dark eyes.

Male: glossy black bird, chocolate brown head

Juvenile: similar to female, but dull gray color and has a streaked chest

Nest: no nest; lays eggs in the nests of other birds

Eggs: 5-7; white with brown markings

Incubation: 10-13 days; host bird incubates eggs

Fledging: 10-11 days; host birds feed young

Migration: partial to non-migrator in New Hampshire and Vermont

Food: insects, seeds; will come to seed feeders

Compare: The female Red-winged Blackbird (pg. 151) is slightly larger and has white eyebrows and a streaked chest. European Starling (pg. 29) is the same size as Brown-headed Cowbird, but it has speckles and a shorter tail.

Stan's Notes: Member of the blackbird family. Of approximately 750 species of parasitic birds worldwide, this is the only parasitic bird in New Hampshire and Vermont, laying eggs in host birds' nests, leaving others to raise its young. Cowbirds are known to have laid eggs in the nests of over 200 species of birds. Some birds reject cowbird eggs, but most will incubate them and raise the young, even to the exclusion of their own. Look for warblers and other birds feeding young birds twice their own size. At one time cowbirds followed bison to feed on insects attracted to the animals.

1 year old

Bohemian
Waxwing

YEAR-ROUND

Cedar Waxwing
Bombycilla cedrorum

Size: 7½" (19 cm)

Male: Very sleek-looking gray-to-brown bird with a pointed crest, light yellow belly and bandit-like black mask. Tip of tail is bright yellow. Red wing tips look like they were dipped in red wax.

Female: same as male

Juvenile: grayish with a heavily streaked chest, lacks red wing tips, black mask and sleek look

Nest: cup; female and male construct; 1 brood per year, occasionally 2

Eggs: 4-6; pale blue with brown markings

Incubation: 10-12 days; female incubates

Fledging: 14-18 days; female and male feed young

Migration: partial to non-migrator; moves to find food

Food: cedar cones, fruit, insects

Compare: Female Northern Cardinal (pg. 149) has a large red bill. The Cedar Waxwing's larger, less common cousin, Bohemian Waxwing (see inset), has white on its wings and rust under its tail.

Stan's Notes: The name is derived from its red wax-like wing tips and preference for the small, blueberry-like cones of the cedar. Mostly seen in flocks, moving around from area to area, looking for berries. Feeds on insects during summer, before berries are abundant. Wanders during winter to find available food supplies. Spends most of its time at the top of tall trees. Listen for the high-pitched "sreee" whistling sounds it constantly makes. Obtains its mask after its first year and red wing tips after the second year.

Wood Thrush
Hylocichla mustelina

Size: 8" (20 cm)

Male: Reddish brown head, back and wings with color fading into a brown tail. A distinctive white breast, belly and sides, covered with black spots. White ring around black eyes, obvious on a black-streaked white face.

Female: same as male

Juvenile: similar to adult

Nest: cup; female builds; 1-2 broods per year

Eggs: 2-4; greenish blue without markings

Incubation: 13-14 days; female incubates

Fledging: 11-12 days; female and male feed young

Migration: complete, to Central and South America

Food: insects, fruit

Compare: Similar body shape as the American Robin (pg. 243), but lacks the Robin's red breast. Larger than Hermit Thrush (pg. 133), with a heavily streaked face. Similar rusty color as Brown Thrasher (pg. 159), but the Thrasher has a much longer rusty red tail and bright yellow eyes unlike the shorter brown tail and black eyes of Wood Thrush.

Stan's Notes: An easy thrush to identify due to the large dark spots on its breast and belly. Well known for its liquid, flute-like calls heard deep in woodlands in New Hampshire and Vermont. Returns to the same woodlands in the last half of April. Often seen on the ground, hopping around like a robin in search of insects.

winter

breeding

SUMMER

Spotted Sandpiper
Actitis macularius

Size: 8" (20 cm)

Male: Olive brown back. Long bill and long, dull yellow legs. White line over the eyes. Breeding plumage has black spots on a white chest and belly. Winter has a clear chest and belly.

Female: same as male

Juvenile: similar to winter adult, with a darker bill

Nest: ground; male builds; 2 broods per year

Eggs: 3-4; brownish with brown markings

Incubation: 20-24 days; male incubates

Fledging: 17-21 days; male feeds young

Migration: complete, to Florida, Mexico and Central and South America

Food: aquatic insects

Compare: Much smaller than the Greater Yellowlegs (pg. 169). Killdeer (pg. 157) has two black neck bands. Look for the Spotted Sandpiper to bob its tail up and down while standing. Look for breeding Spotted Sandpiper's black spots extending from the chest to the belly.

Stan's Notes: One of the few shorebirds that will dive underwater when pursued. Can fly straight up out of the water. Holds wings in a cup-like arc during flight, rarely lifting them above a horizontal plane. Constantly bobs its tail while standing. Walks as if delicately balanced. Female mates with multiple males and lays eggs in up to five nests. Male incubates and cares for the young. Winter plumage Spotted Sandpipers lack black spots on the chest and belly.

male pg. 291

female

juvenile

Northern Cardinal
Cardinalis cardinalis

YEAR-ROUND

Size: 8-9" (20-22.5 cm)

Female: Buff brown bird with tinges of red on crest and wings, a black mask and large red bill.

Male: red bird with a black mask extending from face down to chin and throat, large red bill and crest

Juvenile: same as female, but with a blackish gray bill

Nest: cup; female builds; 2-3 broods per year

Eggs: 3-4; bluish white with brown markings

Incubation: 12-13 days; female and male incubate

Fledging: 9-10 days; female and male feed young

Migration: non-migrator

Food: seeds, insects, fruit; comes to seed feeders

Compare: The Cedar Waxwing (pg. 143) has a small dark bill. Female Cardinal appears similar to the juvenile Cardinal, but juvenile has a dark bill. Look for the bright red bill of the female Northern Cardinal.

Stan's Notes: A familiar backyard bird. Look for the male feeding the female during courtship. Male feeds young of the first brood by himself while the female builds a second nest. The name comes from the Latin word *cardinalis*, which means "important," as represented by Catholic cardinals in their scarlet priestly garments. Very territorial in spring, it fights its own reflection in a window or other reflective surface. Non-territorial during winter, gathering in small flocks of up to 20 birds. Both the female and male sing and can be heard anytime of year. Listen for its "whata-cheer-cheer-cheer" territorial call in spring.

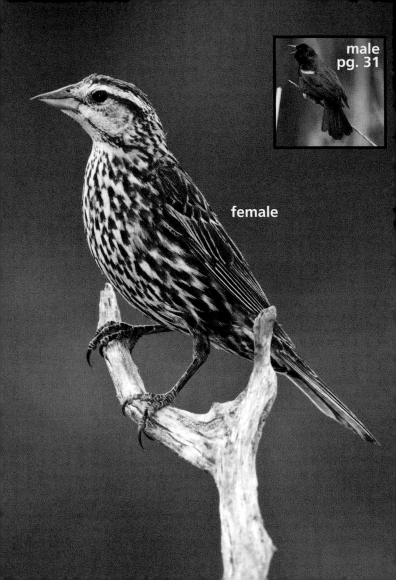

male
pg. 31

female

Red-winged Blackbird
Agelaius phoeniceus

YEAR-ROUND
SUMMER

Size: 8½" (22 cm)

Female: Heavily streaked brown bird with a pointed brown bill and white eyebrows.

Male: jet-black bird with red and yellow patches on upper wings, pointed black bill

Juvenile: same as female

Nest: cup; female builds; 2-3 broods per year

Eggs: 3-4; bluish green with brown markings

Incubation: 10-12 days; female incubates

Fledging: 11-14 days; female and male feed young

Migration: complete, to southeastern New Hampshire, southern states, Mexico and Central America

Food: seeds, insects; will come to seed feeders

Compare: Female Rose-breasted Grosbeak (pg. 137) is similar, but female Red-winged has a thinner body and pointed bill. Female Brown-headed Cowbird (pg. 141) lacks white eyebrows and a heavily streaked chest.

Stan's Notes: One of the most widespread and numerous birds in New Hampshire and Vermont. It's a sure sign of spring when these birds return to the marshes. Flocks with as many as 10,000 birds have been reported. Males arrive before females and defend their territories by singing from the top of surrounding vegetation. Male repeats his call from cattail tops while showing off his red and yellow shoulder patches. Female chooses a mate and often nests over shallow water in thick stands of cattails. Can be aggressive when defending the nest. Feeds mostly on seeds in fall and spring, switching to insects in summer.

male

female

Common Nighthawk
Chordeiles minor

Size: 9" (22.5 cm)

Male: Camouflaged brown and white bird with a white chin. A distinctive white band across the wings and tail, seen only in flight.

Female: similar to male, but with a tan chin, lacks a white tail band

Juvenile: similar to female

Nest: no nest; lays eggs on the ground, usually on rocks or a rooftop; 1 brood per year

Eggs: 2; cream with lavender markings

Incubation: 19-20 days; female and male incubate

Fledging: 20-21 days; female and male feed young

Migration: complete, to South America

Food: insects caught in air

Compare: Much larger than Chimney Swift (pg. 101). Look for the obvious white wing band of the Nighthawk in flight, and the characteristic flap-flap-flap-glide pattern.

Stan's Notes: Usually only seen flying at dusk or after sunset, but it is not uncommon for it to be seen sitting on a branch, sleeping during the day. Very noisy bird, repeating a "peenting" call during flight. Alternates slow wing beats with bursts of quick wing beats. A prolific insect eater. Prefers gravel rooftops for nesting in cities, but these populations are decreasing as flat-topped roofs covered in gravel are converted to regular roofs. Nests on the ground in the country. The male's distinctive mating ritual in spring is a steep diving flight ending with a loud popping noise. One of the first birds to migrate in autumn. Seen in large flocks, all heading south.

in flight

juvenile

male

female

in flight
juvenile

American Kestrel
Falco sparverius

Size: 9-11" (22.5-28 cm); up to 2-foot wingspan

Male: Rusty brown back and tail. White breast with dark spots. Two vertical black lines on a white face. Blue gray wings. Distinctive wide black band with a white edge on tip of a rusty tail.

Female: similar to male, but slightly larger, has rusty brown wings and dark bands on tail

Juvenile: same as adult of the same sex

Nest: cavity; doesn't build a nest within; 1 brood

Eggs: 4-5; white with brown markings

Incubation: 29-31 days; male and female incubate

Fledging: 30-31 days; female and male feed young

Migration: non-migrator to partial in New Hampshire and Vermont

Food: insects, small mammals and birds, reptiles

Compare: Peregrine Falcon (pg. 259) is larger and has a dark "hood" and mustache mark. Look for two vertical black stripes on the Kestrel's face. No other small bird of prey has a rusty back and tail.

Stan's Notes: A falcon that was once called Sparrow Hawk due to its small size. Could be called Grasshopper Hawk because it eats many grasshoppers. Can see ultraviolet light; this helps it locate mice and other small mammals by their urine, which glows bright yellow in ultraviolet light. Hovers near roads, then dives for prey. Adapts quickly to a wooden nest box. Has pointed, swept-back wings, seen in flight. Perches nearly upright. An unusual raptor in that males and females have quite different markings. Watch for them to pump their tails up and down after landing on perches.

Killdeer
Charadrius vociferus

SUMMER

Size: 11" (28 cm)

Male: An upland shorebird with two black bands around the neck like a necklace. Brown back and white belly. Bright reddish orange rump, visible in flight.

Female: same as male

Juvenile: similar to adult, with a single neck band

Nest: ground; male builds; 2 broods per year

Eggs: 3-5; tan with brown markings

Incubation: 24-28 days; male and female incubate

Fledging: 25 days; male and female lead their young to food

Migration: complete, to southern states, Mexico and Central America

Food: insects

Compare: The Spotted Sandpiper (pg. 147) is found around water and lacks the two neck bands of the Killdeer.

Stan's Notes: The only shorebird with two black neck bands. It is known for its broken wing impression, which draws intruders away from the nest. Once clear of the nest, the Killdeer takes flight. Nests are just a slight depression in a gravel area, often very hard to see. Young look like miniature adults on stilts when first hatched. They are able to follow their parents and peck for insects soon after birth. Technically classified as a shorebird but doesn't live at the shore. Often seen in vacant fields or by railroads. Migrates in small flocks. Gives a very distinctive "kill-deer" call.

SUMMER

Brown Thrasher
Toxostoma rufum

Size: 11" (28 cm)

Male: Rusty red bird with a long tail and heavily streaked breast and belly. Two white wing bars. Long curved bill. Bright yellow eyes.

Female: same as male

Juvenile: same as adult, but eye color is grayish

Nest: cup; female and male construct; 2 broods per year

Eggs: 4-5; pale blue with brown markings

Incubation: 11-14 days; female and male incubate

Fledging: 10-13 days; female and male feed young

Migration: complete, to southern states

Food: insects, fruit

Compare: Slightly larger in size and similar in shape to the American Robin (pg. 243) and Gray Catbird (pg. 241), but Brown Thrasher has a streaked chest, rusty color and yellow eyes. The Hermit Thrush (pg. 133) has a shorter brown tail and black eyes. Fox Sparrow has a similar rusty color (pg. 131), but Thrasher is larger and thinner.

Stan's Notes: A prodigious songster, often in thick shrubs where it sings deliberate musical phrases, repeating each twice. Male has the largest documented song repertoire of all North American birds, with over 1,100 song types. Nests low in dense shrubs, often in fencerows. Often seen quickly flying or running in and out of dense shrubs. Noisy feeding due to its habit of turning over leaves, small rocks and branches. More abundant in the central Great Plains than anywhere else in North America.

male

female

Northern Flicker
Colaptes auratus

**YEAR-ROUND
SUMMER**

Size: 12" (30 cm)

Male: Brown and black woodpecker with a large white rump patch, visible only when flying. Black necklace above a speckled breast. Red spot on nape of neck. Black mustache.

Female: same as male, but lacks a black mustache

Juvenile: same as adult of the same sex

Nest: cavity; female and male excavate; 1 brood per year

Eggs: 5-8; white without markings

Incubation: 11-14 days; female and male incubate

Fledging: 25-28 days; female and male feed young

Migration: complete to partial migrator in New Hampshire and Vermont; will move around during winter in search of food

Food: insects, especially ants and beetles

Compare: The male Yellow-bellied Sapsucker (pg. 51) has a red chin. Male Red-bellied Woodpecker (pg. 55) has a red cap and lacks a mustache. Flickers are the only brown-backed woodpeckers in New Hampshire and Vermont.

Stan's Notes: This is the only woodpecker to regularly feed on the ground. Prefers ants and beetles and produces an antacid saliva that neutralizes the acidic defense of ants. Male often picks the nest site; parents take up to 12 days to excavate a hole. Can be attracted with a nest box stuffed with sawdust; often reuses an old nest. Undulates deeply in flight, flashes yellow under the wings and tail and calls "wacka-wacka" loudly.

Mourning Dove
Zenaida macroura

YEAR-ROUND
SUMMER

Size: 12" (30 cm)

Male: Smooth fawn-colored dove. Gray patch on the head. Iridescent pink and greenish blue on neck. Single black spot behind and below eyes. Black spots on wings and tail. Pointed wedge-shaped tail with white edges.

Female: similar to male, lacking iridescent pink and green neck feathers

Juvenile: spotted and streaked

Nest: platform; female and male build; 2 broods per year

Eggs: 2; white without markings

Incubation: 13-14 days; male and female incubate, male incubates during the day, female at night

Fledging: 12-14 days; female and male feed young

Migration: partial migrator to complete; moves around to find food

Food: seeds; will visit seed and ground feeders

Compare: Lacks the black collar and squared tail of the Eurasian Collared-Dove (pg. 253). Smaller than the Rock Pigeon (pg. 255) and lacks its wide range of color combinations.

Stan's Notes: Name comes from its mournful cooing. A ground feeder, bobbing its head as it walks. One of the few birds to drink without lifting its head, same as Rock Pigeon. Parents feed young (squab) a regurgitated liquid called crop-milk the first few days of life. Flimsy platform nest of twigs often falls apart in storms. Wind rushing through its wing feathers during takeoff and flight creates a characteristic whistling sound.

winter

breeding

Pied-billed Grebe
Podilymbus podiceps

SUMMER

Size: 13" (33 cm)

Male: Small brown water bird with a black chin and black ring around a thick, chicken-like ivory bill. Puffy white patch under the tail. Has an unmarked brown bill during winter.

Female: same as male

Juvenile: paler than adult, with white spots and gray chest, belly and bill

Nest: floating platform; female and male construct; 1 brood per year

Eggs: 5-7; bluish white without markings

Incubation: 22-24 days; female and male incubate

Fledging: 45-60 days; female and male feed young

Migration: complete, to southern states, Mexico and Central America

Food: crayfish, aquatic insects, fish

Compare: Look for a puffy white patch under the tail and thick, chicken-like bill to help identify.

Stan's Notes: A common summer resident water bird, often seen diving for food. Slowly sinks like a submarine when disturbed. Sinks without diving by quickly compressing its feathers to force the air out. Was called Hell-diver because of the length of time it can stay submerged. Can surface far from where it went under. Very sensitive to pollution. Well suited to life on water, with short wings, lobed toes, and legs set close to the rear of its body. While swimming is easy, it is very awkward on land. Builds nest on a floating mat in water. "Grebe" probably came from the Old English word *krib*, meaning "crest," a reference to the crested head plumes of many grebes, especially during breeding season.

male pg. 59

female

Bufflehead
Bucephala albeola

Size: 13-15" (33-38 cm)

Female: Brownish gray duck with a dark brown head. White patch on cheek, just behind eyes.

Male: striking black and white duck, head shines green purple in sunlight, large white bonnet-like patch on back of head

Juvenile: similar to female

Nest: cavity; female lines an old woodpecker cavity; 1 brood per year

Eggs: 8-10; ivory to olive without markings

Incubation: 29-31 days; female incubates

Fledging: 50-55 days; female leads young to food

Migration: complete, to New Hampshire and Vermont, southern states, Mexico and Central America

Food: aquatic insects

Compare: Slightly smaller than the female Lesser Scaup (pg. 177), which has a white patch at the base of its bill that is unlike the female Bufflehead's white patch on the cheek.

Stan's Notes: This very small, common duck is almost always in small groups or with other ducks. A diving duck, seen on rivers and lakes in New Hampshire and Vermont during migration and winter. Nests in old woodpecker holes. Known to use a burrow in an earthen bank when tree cavities are scarce. Will use a nest box. Uses down feathers to line the nest cavity. Unlike other ducks, the young remain in the nest for up to two days before venturing out with their mothers. Female is very territorial and stays with the same mate for many years.

Greater Yellowlegs
Tringa melanoleuca

MIGRATION

Size: 14" (36 cm)

Male: Tall bird with a bulbous head and long thin bill, slightly upturned. Gray streaking on the chest. White belly. Long yellow legs.

Female: same as male

Juvenile: same as adult

Nest: ground; female builds; 1 brood per year

Eggs: 3-4; off-white with brown markings

Incubation: 22-23 days; female and male incubate

Fledging: 18-20 days; male and female feed young

Migration: complete, to southern states, Mexico and Central and South America

Food: small fish, aquatic insects

Compare: Larger than the Killdeer (pg. 157) and lacks the two black bands around the neck. Larger than Spotted Sandpiper (pg. 147), which has a spotted chest during breeding season.

Stan's Notes: A common shorebird seen during migration. Can be identified by its long yellow legs, which carry it through deep water, and the slightly upturned bill. Often seen resting on one leg. Feeds by rushing forward through the water, plowing its bill or swinging it from side to side, catching small fish and insects. A skittish bird quick to give an alarm call, causing flocks to take flight. Quite often moves into the water prior to taking flight. Has a variety of "flight" notes that it gives when taking off. Nests on the ground close to water on the northern tundra of Labrador and Newfoundland.

Green-winged Teal
Anas crecca

MIGRATION
WINTER

Size: 15" (38 cm)

Male: A chestnut head with a dark green patch in back of eyes extending down to the nape of neck and outlined in white. Gray body. Butter yellow tail. Green patch on wings (speculum), seen in flight.

Female: light brown duck with black spots and green speculum, small black bill

Juvenile: same as female

Nest: ground; female builds; 1 brood per year

Eggs: 8-10; creamy white without markings

Incubation: 21-23 days; female incubates

Fledging: 32-34 days; female teaches young to feed

Migration: complete, to southeastern New Hampshire, southern states

Food: aquatic plants and insects

Compare: The female Blue-winged Teal (pg. 173) is similar in size, but it has slight white at the base of bill. Look for a dark green patch on each side of a chestnut head to identify the male Green-winged Teal.

Stan's Notes: One of the smallest dabbling ducks, it tips forward in the water to feed off the bottom of shallow ponds. This behavior makes it vulnerable to ingesting spent lead shot, which can cause death. It walks well on land and also feeds in fields and woodlands. Known for its fast and agile flight, groups spin and wheel through the air in tight formation. Green speculum on wings most obvious in flight.

Blue-winged Teal
Spatula discors

MIGRATION
SUMMER

Size: 15-16" (38-40 cm)

Male: Small, plain-looking brown duck with black speckles. Large white crescent-shaped mark at the base of bill. Gray head. Black tail with a small white patch. Blue wing patch (speculum), usually seen only in flight.

Female: duller version of male, lacks a crescent mark on the face and white patch on tail, showing only slight white at the base of bill

Juvenile: same as female

Nest: ground; female builds; 1 brood per year

Eggs: 8-11; creamy white

Incubation: 23-27 days; female incubates

Fledging: 35-44 days; female feeds young

Migration: complete, to southern states, Mexico and Central America

Food: aquatic plants, seeds, aquatic insects

Compare: Male Blue-winged Teal has a white mark on its face. Female Green-winged Teal (pg. 171) lacks white at the base of bill. Female Mallard (pg. 197) and female Wood Duck (pg. 189) are larger, and the Wood Duck has a crest.

Stan's Notes: One of the smallest ducks in North America and one of the longest distance migrating ducks. Widespread nesting, as far north as Alaska. Builds nest some distance from the water. Female performs a distraction display to protect the nest and young. Male leaves the female near the end of incubation. Planting crops and cultivating to pond edges have caused declining populations.

173

YEAR-ROUND

Spruce Grouse
Falcipennis canadensis

Size: 16" (40 cm); up to 2-foot wingspan

Male: Plump grouse, brown to almost black, with white speckles on the chest and belly. Short neck, red eyebrows (combs) and short dark tail with a chestnut tip.

Female: overall brown grouse with small black and white barring on the chest, dark brown tail with a chestnut tip

Juvenile: similar to female

Nest: ground; female builds; 1 brood per year

Eggs: 4-7; tan with brown markings

Incubation: 17-24 days; female incubates

Fledging: 8-10 days; male and female feed young

Migration: non-migrator; moves around to find food

Food: coniferous needles, insects, seeds, berries

Compare: The Ruffed Grouse (pg. 185) is lighter brown with a lighter-colored tail and has a tuft of feathers on its head.

Stan's Notes: Well known for being semi-tame and approachable. In winter it is often seen in groups along roads, where snow isn't as deep and small rocks can be eaten to aid in digestion. Prefers open coniferous forests. Eats mainly spruce needles, hence its common name. Roosts in trees. Displaying male fans its tail, leans forward, droops its wings and quickly flaps a short flight. Female is territorial against other females. The cryptic coloring of the female allows her to blend in with the surroundings. Often freezes when danger approaches, hence its other common name, Fool Hen.

male pg. 61

female

Lesser Scaup
Aythya affinis

MIGRATION
WINTER

Size: 16-17" (40-43 cm)

Female: Overall brown duck with a dull white patch at the base of a light gray bill. Yellow eyes.

Male: white and gray duck, chest and head appear nearly black but the head looks purple with green highlights in direct sun, yellow eyes

Juvenile: same as female

Nest: ground; female builds; 1 brood per year

Eggs: 8-14; olive buff without markings

Incubation: 22-28 days; female incubates

Fledging: 45-50 days; female teaches young to feed

Migration: complete, to southeastern New Hampshire, southern states

Food: aquatic plants and insects

Compare: Female Ring-necked Duck (pg. 179) has a white ring on its bill. Male Blue-winged Teal (pg. 173) has a crescent-shaped white mark at the base of its bill. The female Wood Duck (pg. 189) is larger with white around its eyes.

Stan's Notes: A diving duck seen during migration and winter. Often in large flocks numbering in the thousands on lakes, ponds and along the coast. Submerges itself completely to feed on the bottom of lakes (unlike dabbling ducks, which only tip forward to reach the bottom). Note the bold white stripe under the wings when in flight. Male leaves the female when she starts incubating eggs. The quantity of eggs (clutch size) increases with the age of the female. This species has an interesting baby-sitting arrangement in which groups of young (crèches) are tended by 1-3 adult females.

male pg. 63

female

Ring-necked Duck
Aythya collaris

MIGRATION
SUMMER

Size: 17" (43 cm)

Female: Mainly brown back with light brown sides, a gray face and dark brown crown. White eye-ring extends into a line behind the eye. White ring around a light blue bill. Top of head is peaked.

Male: black head, breast and back, sides are gray to nearly white, a bold white ring around a light blue bill and second ring at the base of bill, top of head is peaked

Juvenile: similar to female

Nest: ground; female builds; 1 brood per year

Eggs: 8-10; olive gray to brown without markings

Incubation: 26-27 days; female incubates

Fledging: 49-56 days; female teaches young to feed

Migration: complete, to southern states

Food: aquatic plants and insects

Compare: Female Lesser Scaup (pg. 177) is similar in size. Look for the white ring around the bill of the female Ring-necked Duck.

Stan's Notes: A summer resident and migrator in New Hampshire and Vermont. Usually seen in larger freshwater lakes. A diving duck, watch for it to dive underwater to forage for food. Takes to flight by springing up off the water. Was named "Ring-necked" for its cinnamon-colored collar (nearly impossible to see in the field). Also called Ring-billed Duck due to the white ring on its bill.

soaring

Broad-winged Hawk
Buteo platypterus

SUMMER

Size: 15-19" (38-48 cm); up to 3-foot wingspan

Male: Slightly smaller than the American Crow. A brown back and rusty red bars on the chest. Two to three wide black-and-white tail bands. White under the wings and black "fingertips," seen in flight.

Female: same as male

Juvenile: tail bands narrower and more numerous, a brown-streaked chest and belly

Nest: platform; female and male build, but female finishes; 1 brood per year

Eggs: 2-3; off-white with brown markings

Incubation: 28-32 days; female incubates, male feeds the female during incubation

Fledging: 34-40 days; female and male feed young

Migration: complete, to Central and South America

Food: small birds, small mammals, snakes, frogs, toads, large insects

Compare: Similar in size to Cooper's Hawk (pg. 257), but has a wider, shorter tail. Larger than the Sharp-shinned Hawk (pg. 251). Look for the alternating black-and-white tail bands.

Stan's Notes: A very common woodland hawk in New Hampshire and Vermont. Can be seen in large groups (kettles) migrating early in autumn. Spends most of its time hunting small birds, snakes and frogs in dense woodlands. Propels itself through dense woods with its short, round wings. Screams a high-pitched whistle call repetitively when intruders are near the nest.

soaring

Red-shouldered Hawk
Buteo lineatus

Size: 15-19" (38-48 cm); up to 3½-foot wingspan

Male: Reddish (cinnamon) head, shoulders, breast and belly. Wings and back are dark brown with white spots. Long tail with thin white bands and wide black bands. Obvious red wing linings, seen in flight.

Female: same as male

Juvenile: similar to adult, lacks the cinnamon color, has a white chest with dark spots

Nest: platform; female and male construct; 1 brood per year

Eggs: 2-4; white with dark markings

Incubation: 27-29 days; female and male incubate

Fledging: 39-45 days; female feeds young

Migration: complete, to southern states, partial migrator in New Hampshire

Food: reptiles, amphibians, large insects, birds

Compare: Red-tailed Hawk (pg. 203) has a white chest. The Sharp-shinned Hawk (pg. 251) is smaller and lacks the reddish head and belly of the Red-shouldered Hawk.

Stan's Notes: Common woodland hawk in New Hampshire and Vermont. Seen in backyards. Likes to hunt at forest edges, spotting snakes, frogs, insects, an occasional small bird and other prey as it perches. Often flaps with an alternating gliding pattern. Very vocal with a distinct scream. Breeds when it reaches 2-3 years. Remains in the same territory for many years. Starts constructing its nest in March or April. Young leave the nest in June or July.

drumming

Ruffed Grouse
Bonasa umbellus

YEAR-ROUND

Size: 16-19" (40-48 cm); up to 2-foot wingspan

Male: Brown chicken-like bird with a long squared tail. Wide black band near tip of tail. Is able to fan tail like a turkey. Tuft of feathers on the head stands like a crown. Black ruffs on sides of neck.

Female: same as male, but less obvious neck ruffs

Juvenile: same as female

Nest: ground; female builds; 1 brood per year

Eggs: 9-12; tan with light brown markings

Incubation: 23-24 days; female incubates

Fledging: 10-12 days; female leads young to food

Migration: non-migrator; moves around to find food

Food: seeds, insects, fruit, leaf buds

Compare: Female Ring-necked Pheasant (pg. 211) is larger and has a longer, pointed tail. Spruce Grouse (pg. 175) has a darker tail. Look for a feathered tuft on the head and black neck ruffs to help identify the Ruffed Grouse.

Stan's Notes: A common bird of deep woods. Often seen in aspen or other trees, feeding on leaf buds. In the more northern climates, bristles grow on its feet in winter, which serve as snowshoes. When there is enough snow, it will dive into a snowbank to roost at night. In spring, the male raises its crest (tuft), fans tail feathers and stands on logs, drumming with its wings to attract females. The drumming sound comes from its cupped wings moving air, not from pounding against its chest or a log. Female performs a distraction display to protect her young. Two color morphs, red and gray, most apparent in the tail. Black ruffs on the neck gave rise to its common name.

male pg. 65

female

Hooded Merganser
Lophodytes cucullatus

YEAR-ROUND
SUMMER

Size: 16-19" (40-48 cm)

Female: Sleek brown and rust bird with a red head. Ragged "hair" on back of head. A long, thin brown bill. Yellow-to-gold eyes.

Male: same size and shape as female, but a black back and rusty sides, crest "hood" raises to show off a large white patch, long black bill

Juvenile: similar to female, brown eyes

Nest: cavity; female lines an old woodpecker cavity; 1 brood per year

Eggs: 10-12; white without markings

Incubation: 32-33 days; female incubates

Fledging: 71 days; female feeds young

Migration: complete to partial migrator in New Hampshire and Vermont

Food: small fish, aquatic insects

Compare: The female Lesser Scaup (pg. 177) is slightly smaller and has a dull white patch at the base of its bill.

Stan's Notes: Small diving bird of shallow ponds, sloughs, lakes and rivers. The male Hoodie voluntarily raises and lowers his crest "hood" to show off his large white head patch. Rarely found away from wooded areas, where it nests in natural cavities or nest boxes. The female will "dump" her eggs in other Hoodie or Wood Duck nests, which results in 20-25 eggs in some nests. Known to share nest cavities with Common Goldeneyes and Wood Ducks, sitting side by side.

male pg. 269

female

Wood Duck
Aix sponsa

SUMMER

Size: 17-20" (43-50 cm)

Female: A small brown dabbling duck. Bright white eye-ring and not-so-obvious crest. Blue patch on wing, often hidden.

Male: highly ornamented with green head and crest patterned with white and black, rusty chest, white belly and red eyes

Juvenile: similar to female

Nest: cavity; female lines an old woodpecker cavity; 1 brood per year

Eggs: 10-15; creamy white without markings

Incubation: 28-36 days; female incubates

Fledging: 56-68 days; female teaches young to feed

Migration: complete, to southern states

Food: aquatic insects, plants, seeds

Compare: Female Mallard (pg. 197) and female Blue-winged Teal (pg. 173) lack the bright white eye-ring and crest. Female Northern Shoveler (pg. 195) has a large spoon-shaped bill.

Stan's Notes: Common duck of quiet, shallow backwater ponds. Nearly extinct around 1900 from overhunting but doing well now. Nests in an old woodpecker cavity or uses a nest box. Often seen flying deep in forests or perched high on tree branches. Female takes to flight with a loud squealing call and enters nest cavity from full flight. Lays eggs in a neighboring female nest (egg dumping), resulting in excess of 20 eggs in some clutches. Young stay in nest 24 hours after hatching, then jump from up to 60 feet (18 m) to the ground or water to follow their mother, never returning to the nest.

female

male pg. 67

Common Goldeneye
Bucephala clangula

MIGRATION
SUMMER
WINTER

Size:	18½-19½" (47-49.5 cm)
Female:	A brown and gray duck with a large dark brown head and gray body. White collar. Bright golden eyes. Yellow-tipped dark bill.
Male:	mostly white duck with a black back and a large, puffy green head, large white spot in front of each bright golden eye, dark bill
Juvenile:	same as female, but has a dark bill
Nest:	cavity; female lines an old woodpecker cavity; 1 brood per year
Eggs:	8-10; light green without markings
Incubation:	28-32 days; female incubates
Fledging:	56-59 days; female leads young to food
Migration:	complete, to southeastern New Hampshire, southern states, Mexico
Food:	aquatic plants, insects, fish, mollusks
Compare:	Female Lesser Scaup (pg. 177) has a white patch at the base of its bill. Look for the large dark brown head and white collar to identify the female Common Goldeneye.

Stan's Notes: Known for its loud whistling in flight, produced by its wings. In late winter and early spring, the male often attracts a female through elaborate displays, throwing his head back while uttering a raspy note. Female will lay eggs in other goldeneye nests, resulting in some mothers incubating up to 30 eggs. Received the common name from its obvious bright golden eyes.

American Wigeon
Anas americana

MIGRATION
SUMMER
WINTER

Size: 19" (48 cm)

Male: A brown duck with a rounded head, a long pointed tail and short, black-tipped grayish bill. Obvious white cap. Deep green patch starting behind eyes, streaking down neck. White belly and wing linings, seen in flight. Non-breeding lacks white cap, green patch.

Female: light brown with a pale gray head, a short, black-tipped grayish bill, green wing patch (speculum), dark eye spot, white belly and wing linings, seen in flight

Juvenile: similar to female

Nest: ground; female builds; 1 brood per year

Eggs: 7-12; white without markings

Incubation: 23-25 days; female incubates

Fledging: 37-48 days; female teaches young to feed

Migration: complete, to southeastern New Hampshire, southern states, Mexico

Food: aquatic plants, seeds

Compare: Male American Wigeon is easily identified by the white cap and black-tipped grayish bill. Look for the black-tipped grayish bill and green wing patch to help identify the female American Wigeon.

Stan's Notes: Often in small flocks or with other ducks. Prefers shallow lakes. Male stays with the female only during the first week of incubation. Female raises the young. If threatened, female feigns injury while the young run and hide. Conceals upland nest in tall vegetation within 50-250 yards (46-229 m) of water.

193

male pg. 273

female

MIGRATION
WINTER

Northern Shoveler
Spatula clypeata

Size:	20" (50 cm)
Female:	A medium-sized brown duck speckled with black. Green speculum. An extraordinarily large, spoon-shaped bill that is almost always held pointed toward the water.
Male:	iridescent green head, rusty sides and white breast, spoon-shaped bill
Juvenile:	same as female
Nest:	ground; female builds; 1 brood per year
Eggs:	9-12; olive without markings
Incubation:	22-25 days; female incubates
Fledging:	30-60 days; female leads young to food
Migration:	complete, to southeastern New Hampshire, southern states, Mexico and Central America
Food:	aquatic insects, plants
Compare:	Similar color as female Mallard (pg. 197), but Mallard lacks the Shoveler's large bill. Female Wood Duck (pg. 189) is smaller and has a white eye-ring. Look for the Shoveler's large spoon-shaped bill to help identify.

Stan's Notes: One of several species of shoveler, so called because of the peculiar shape of its bill. The first part of the common name was given because this is the only species of these ducks in North America. Found in small flocks of 5-10 birds, swimming low in water, pointing its large bill toward the water as if it's too heavy to lift. Feeds mainly by filtering tiny aquatic insects and plants from the surface of the water with its bill, often swimming in tight circles while feeding.

male pg. 275

female

Mallard
Anas platyrhynchos

YEAR-ROUND

Size: 19-21" (48-53 cm)

Female: Brown duck with an orange and black bill and blue and white wing mark (speculum).

Male: large, bulbous green head, white necklace, rust brown or chestnut chest, combination of gray and white on the sides, yellow bill, orange legs and feet

Juvenile: same as female, but with a yellow bill

Nest: ground; female builds; 1 brood per year

Eggs: 7-10; greenish to whitish, unmarked

Incubation: 26-30 days; female incubates

Fledging: 42-52 days; female leads young to food

Migration: partial to non-migrator in New Hampshire and Vermont

Food: seeds, plants, aquatic insects; will come to ground feeders offering corn

Compare: Female Shoveler (pg. 195) is smaller and has a large spoon-shaped bill. The female Wood Duck (pg. 189) has a white eye-ring. Female Blue-winged Teal (pg. 173) is smaller than the female Mallard.

Stan's Notes: A familiar duck of lakes and ponds, it's considered a type of dabbling duck, tipping forward in shallow water to feed on aquatic plants on the bottom. The name "Mallard" comes from the Latin *masculus*, meaning "male," referring to the habit of males not taking part in raising ducklings. Both female and male have white tails and white underwings. Black central tail feathers of male curl upward. Will return to place of birth.

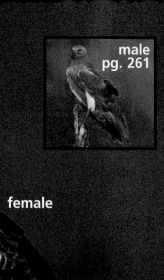

male
pg. 261

female

soaring

Northern Harrier
Circus hudsonius

YEAR-ROUND
SUMMER

Size: 18-22" (45-56 cm); up to 4-foot wingspan

Female: A slim, low-flying hawk. Dark brown back with a brown-streaked chest and belly. Large white rump patch and narrow black bands across tail. Black wing tips. Yellow eyes.

Male: silver gray with a large white rump patch and white belly, faint narrow bands across tail, black wing tips, yellow eyes

Juvenile: similar to female, with an orange chest

Nest: ground; female and male construct; 1 brood per year

Eggs: 4-8; bluish white without markings

Incubation: 31-32 days; female incubates

Fledging: 30-35 days; male and female feed young

Migration: complete to partial migrator in New Hampshire and Vermont

Food: mice, snakes, insects, small birds

Compare: Slimmer than the Red-tailed Hawk (pg. 203). Look for black tail bands, a white rump patch and the characteristic flight to help identify.

Stan's Notes: One of the easiest of hawks to identify. Glides just aboveground, following the contours of the land while searching for prey. Holds its wings just above the horizontal position, tilting back and forth in the wind, similar to Turkey Vultures. Formerly called Marsh Hawk due to its habit of hunting over marshes. Feeds on the ground. Will perch on the ground to preen and rest. Unlike other hawks, uses its hearing primarily to locate prey, followed by eyesight. At any age, it has a distinctive owl-like face disk.

dark
morph

light morph

soaring dark
morph

soaring light
morph

Rough-legged Hawk
Buteo lagopus

WINTER

Size: 18-23" (45-58 cm); up to 4½-foot wingspan

Male: A hawk of several plumages. All have a long tail with a dark band or bands, relatively long wings, and a small bill and feet. Distinctive dark "wrists" and belly. Light morph has a nearly pure white underside of wings and base of tail. Dark morph is nearly all brown with a light gray trailing edge of wings.

Female: same as male, only larger

Juvenile: same as adults

Nest: platform, on edge of cliff; female and male build; 1 brood per year

Eggs: 2-6; white without markings

Incubation: 28-31 days; female and male incubate

Fledging: 39-43 days; female and male feed young

Migration: complete, to the northern half of the U.S.

Food: small mammals, snakes, large insects

Compare: Red-tailed Hawk (pg. 203) has a belly band and lacks dark "wrist" marks. The Osprey (pg. 73) has similar dark "wrists," but lacks the dark belly of the Rough-legged Hawk.

Stan's Notes: Two color morphs; light is more common than the dark. A common resident during winter, nesting in the Canadian Northwest Territories and Alaska. More numerous in some years than in others. It has much smaller, weaker feet than other birds of prey and must hunt smaller prey. Hunts from the air, usually hovering before diving for mice, voles and other small rodents.

soaring

Red-tailed Hawk
Buteo jamaicensis

Size: 19-23" (48-58 cm); up to 4½-foot wingspan

Male: A large hawk with a wide variety of colors from bird to bird, from chocolate brown to nearly all white. Often brown with a white breast and distinctive brown belly band. Rust red tail, usually seen only from above. Wing underside is white with a small dark patch on leading edge near shoulder.

Female: same as male, only slightly larger

Juvenile: similar to adults, lacking the red tail, has a speckled chest and light eyes

Nest: platform; male and female construct; 1 brood per year

Eggs: 2-3; white without markings or sometimes marked with brown

Incubation: 30-35 days; female and male incubate

Fledging: 45-46 days; male and female feed young

Migration: non-migrator to partial; will move around in winter to find food

Food: mice, birds, snakes, insects, mammals

Compare: Red-shouldered Hawk (pg. 183) lacks a red tail and white chest. The Sharp-shinned Hawk (pg. 251) is much smaller.

Stan's Notes: Common hawk of open country and in cities, often seen perched on freeway light posts, fences and trees. Look for it circling over open fields and roadsides, searching for prey. Builds a large stick nest; commonly seen in large trees along roads. Lines nest with finer material such as evergreen tree needles. Returns to same nest site each year. Develops the red tail in its second year.

YEAR-ROUND

Barred Owl
Strix varia

Size: 20-24" (50-60 cm); up to 3½-foot wingspan

Male: A chunky brown and gray owl with a large head and dark brown eyes. Dark horizontal barring on upper chest. Vertical streaks on lower chest and belly. Yellow bill and feet.

Female: same as male, only slightly larger

Juvenile: light gray with a black face

Nest: cavity; does not add nesting material; 1 brood per year

Eggs: 2-3; white without markings

Incubation: 28-33 days; female incubates

Fledging: 42-44 days; female and male feed young

Migration: non-migrator

Food: mammals, birds, fish, reptiles, amphibians

Compare: Lacks the "horns" of the Great Horned Owl (pg. 207) and ear tufts of the tiny Eastern Screech-Owl (pg. 237). Eastern Screech-Owl is less than half the size of Barred Owl.

Stan's Notes: A very common owl that can often be seen hunting during the day, perching and watching for mice, birds and other prey. One of the few owls to take fish out of a lake. Prefers dense deciduous woodlands with sparse undergrowth. Can be attracted with a simple nest box with a large opening, attached to a tree. The young stay with their parents for up to four months after fledging. Often sounds like a dog barking just before giving a call of 6-8 hoots that sounds like, "Who-who-who-cooks-for-you?" The hooting call of a Great Horned Owl sounds like, "Hoo-hoo-hoo-hoooo!"

Great Horned Owl
Bubo virginianus

Size: 21-25" (53-63 cm); up to 3½-foot wingspan

Male: A robust brown "horned" owl. Bright yellow eyes and V-shaped white throat resembling a necklace. Horizontal barring on the chest.

Female: same as male, only slightly larger

Juvenile: similar to adults, lacking ear tufts

Nest: no nest; takes over the nest of a crow, Great Blue Heron or hawk, or uses a partial cavity, stump or broken-off tree; 1 brood per year

Eggs: 2-3; white without markings

Incubation: 26-30 days; female incubates

Fledging: 30-35 days; male and female feed young

Migration: non-migrator

Food: mammals, birds (ducks), snakes, insects

Compare: The Barred Owl (pg. 205) has dark eyes and no "horns." Over twice the size of its cousin, the Eastern Screech-Owl (pg. 237). Look for bright yellow eyes and feathers on the head to help identify this bird.

Stan's Notes: The largest owl in New Hampshire and Vermont. A winter nester, laying eggs in January and February. It has excellent hearing; able to hear a mouse move beneath a pile of leaves or a foot of snow. "Ears" are tufts of feathers (horns) and have nothing to do with hearing. Not able to turn its head all the way around. Wing feathers are ragged on the ends, resulting in silent flight. Eyelids close from the top down, like humans. Fearless, it's one of the few animals that will kill a skunk or porcupine. Because of this, it is sometimes called Flying Tiger.

American Black Duck
Anas rubripes

YEAR-ROUND
SUMMER

Size: 23" (58 cm)

Male: Overall dark brown, sometimes appearing nearly black, with a lighter head and neck. A yellow bill and orange legs. Violet patch on the wings (speculum), bordered with black. Dark wings contrast sharply with white wing linings, seen in flight.

Female: same as male, except bill is dull green with black flecks

Juvenile: same as female

Nest: ground; female builds; 1 brood per year

Eggs: 8-10; creamy white to greenish buff

Incubation: 26-29 days; female incubates

Fledging: 16-17 days; female teaches young to feed

Migration: complete to non-migrator in New Hampshire and Vermont

Food: aquatic plants, seeds

Compare: Male and female American Black Ducks are very similar to the female Mallard (pg. 197), but Mallard has an orange bill and a blue wing patch (speculum) bordered with white.

Stan's Notes: Was once one of the most abundant ducks breeding in the United States; now Mallards are more common. Sometimes mates (hybridizes) with Mallards, producing males that lack the brilliant colors of male Mallards. Female constructs a nest in grass that is high enough to conceal. Male leaves the female while she is still incubating eggs. Young leave the nest 1-3 hours after hatching.

male

female

Ring-necked Pheasant
Phasianus colchicus

Size: 30-36" (76-90 cm), male, including tail
21-25" (53-63 cm), female, including tail

Male: Golden brown body with a long tail. White ring around the neck. Head is purple, green, blue and red.

Female: smaller, less flamboyant all-brown bird with a long tail

Juvenile: similar to female, with a shorter tail

Nest: ground; female builds; 1 brood per year

Eggs: 8-10; olive brown without markings

Incubation: 23-25 days; female incubates

Fledging: 11-12 days; female leads young to food

Migration: non-migrator; moves around to find food

Food: insects, seeds, fruit; visits ground feeders

Compare: Male Ring-necked Pheasant is much larger than the female. Both have long tails, but unlike the female Ring-necked, the male is brightly colored.

Stan's Notes: Originally introduced to North America from China in the late 1800s. Common now throughout the United States. Like many other game birds, its numbers vary greatly, making it common during some years and scarce in others. Common name "Ring-necked" refers to the thin white ring around the male's neck. "Pheasant" comes from the Greek *phaisianos*, meaning "bird of the River Phasis." (This river is located in Europe and is now known as the Rioni River.) Listen for the male's cackling call, which attracts females. Roosts on the ground or in trees at night.

displaying male

non-displaying

female

Wild Turkey
Meleagris gallopavo

YEAR-ROUND

Size: 36-48" (90-120 cm)

Male: Large, plump brown and bronze bird with a striking blue and red bare head. Fan tail and a long, straight black beard in center of chest. Spurs on legs.

Female: thinner and less striking than male, usually lacking a breast beard

Juvenile: same as adult of the same sex

Nest: ground; female builds; 1 brood per year

Eggs: 10-12; buff white with dull brown markings

Incubation: 27-28 days; female incubates

Fledging: 6-10 days; female leads young to food

Migration: non-migrator; moves around to find food

Food: insects, seeds, fruit

Compare: This bird is quite distinctive and unlikely to be confused with others.

Stan's Notes: The largest native game bird in New Hampshire and Vermont, and the species from which the domestic turkey was bred. It almost became our national bird, losing to the Bald Eagle by one vote. Eliminated from many eastern states due to market hunting and loss of habitat. Reintroduced widely during the 1960-80s. Populations are now stable. A strong flier that can approach 60 mph (97 km/h). Able to fly straight up, then away. Eyesight is three times better than human eyesight. Hearing is also excellent; can hear competing males up to a mile away. Males hold "harems" of up to 20 females. Males are known as toms, females are hens, young are poults. Roosts in trees at night.

male

female

Golden-crowned Kinglet
Regulus satrapa

Size: 4" (10 cm)

Male: Tiny, plump green-to-gray bird. Distinctive yellow and orange patch with a black border on the crown (see inset). A white eyebrow mark. Two white wing bars.

Female: same as male, but has a yellow crown with a black border, lacks any orange (see inset)

Juvenile: same as adults, but lacks gold on crown

Nest: pendulous; female builds; 1-2 broods per year

Eggs: 5-9; white or creamy with brown markings

Incubation: 14-15 days; female incubates

Fledging: 14-19 days; female and male feed young

Migration: non-migrator in New Hampshire, Vermont

Food: insects, fruit, tree sap

Compare: Similar to Ruby-crowned Kinglet (pg. 217), but Golden-crowned has an obvious crown. Smaller than the female American Goldfinch (pg. 307), which has an all-black forehead.

Stan's Notes: Common year-round resident in New Hampshire and Vermont, but might be seen more often during migration, when flocks from farther north move through. Often in flocks with chickadees, nuthatches, woodpeckers, Brown Creepers and Ruby-crowned Kinglets. Flicks its wings when moving around. Builds an unusual hanging nest, often with moss, lichens and spider webs, and lines it with bark and feathers. Can have so many eggs in its small nest that eggs are in two layers. Drinks tree sap and feeds by gleaning insects from trees. Can be very tame and approachable.

Ruby-crowned Kinglet
Regulus calendula

MIGRATION
SUMMER

Size: 4" (10 cm)

Male: A small, teardrop-shaped green-to-gray bird. Two white wing bars and a white eye-ring. Hidden ruby crown.

Female: same as male, but lacking the ruby crown

Juvenile: same as female

Nest: pendulous; female builds; 1 brood per year

Eggs: 4-5; white with brown markings

Incubation: 11-12 days; female incubates

Fledging: 11-12 days; female and male feed young

Migration: complete, to southern states, Mexico, Central America; some individuals are non-migrators

Food: insects, berries

Compare: Golden-crowned Kinglet (pg. 215) lacks the ruby crown. The female American Goldfinch (pg. 307) shares the same olive color and unmarked breast, but it is larger. Look for the white eye-ring of Ruby-crowned Kinglet.

Stan's Notes: One of the smaller birds found in New Hampshire and Vermont. Most commonly seen during migration, when groups travel together. Watch for it flitting around thick shrubs low to the ground. It takes a quick eye to see the male's ruby crown. Female constructs an unusual pendulous (sac-like) nest, intricately woven and decorated on the outside with colored lichens and mosses stuck together with spider webs. Nest is suspended from a branch overlapped by leaves and usually is hung high in a mature tree. The name "Kinglet" originates from the Anglo-Saxon word *cyning*, or "king," referring to the male's ruby crown, and the diminutive suffix "let," meaning "small."

male

female

YEAR-ROUND

Red-breasted Nuthatch
Sitta canadensis

Size: 4½" (11 cm)

Male: Small gray-backed bird with a black cap and prominent eye line. Rust red chest and belly.

Female: gray cap, pale undersides

Juvenile: same as female

Nest: cavity; male and female excavate; 1 brood per year

Eggs: 5-6; white with red brown markings

Incubation: 11-12 days; female incubates

Fledging: 14-20 days; female and male feed young

Migration: irruptive; moves around in search of food

Food: insects, seeds; visits seed and suet feeders

Compare: Smaller than the White-breasted Nuthatch (pg. 223), with a red chest instead of white.

Stan's Notes: The Red-breasted Nuthatch behaves like the White-breasted Nuthatch, climbing down tree trunks headfirst. Similar to chickadees, visits seed feeders, quickly grabbing a seed and flying off to crack it open. Will wedge a seed into a crevice and pound it open with several sharp blows. The name "Nuthatch" comes from the Middle English moniker *nuthak*, referring to the bird's habit of wedging a seed into a crevice and hacking it open. Look for it in mature conifers, where it often extracts seeds from cones. Excavates a cavity or takes an old woodpecker hole or natural cavity and constructs a nest. Irruptive migration means the bird is common in some winters and scarce in others.

Boreal Chickadee

YEAR-ROUND

Black-capped Chickadee
Poecile atricapillus

Size: 5" (13 cm)

Male: Familiar gray bird with a black cap and throat patch. White chest and tan belly. Small white wing marks.

Female: same as male

Juvenile: same as adult

Nest: cavity; female and male construct or excavate; 1 brood per year

Eggs: 5-7; white with fine brown markings

Incubation: 11-13 days; female and male incubate

Fledging: 14-18 days; female and male feed young

Migration: non-migrator

Food: insects, seeds, fruit; will come to seed and suet feeders

Compare: Tufted Titmouse (pg. 229) is larger than the Black-capped Chickadee and has a crest. The Boreal Chickadee (see inset) is very similar, but it has a brown cap and sides.

Stan's Notes: A backyard bird that is attracted with a nest box or seed feeder. Usually the first to find a new feeder. Can be easily tamed and hand fed. Much of its diet comes from bird feeders, so it can be a common urban bird. Needs to feed each day in winter; forages for food even in the worst winter storms. Often seen with nuthatches, woodpeckers and other birds. Builds nest mostly with green moss and lines it with fur. Named for its familiar "chika-dee-dee-dee-dee" call. Also calls a high-pitched, two-toned "fee-bee." Can have different calls in different regions. Boreal Chickadee is uncommon, seen in northern New Hampshire and Vermont.

YEAR-ROUND

White-breasted Nuthatch
Sitta carolinensis

Size: 5-6" (13-15 cm)

Male: Slate gray with a white face and belly, and black cap and nape. Long thin bill, slightly upturned. Chestnut undertail.

Female: similar to male, gray cap and nape

Juvenile: similar to female

Nest: cavity; female and male construct; 1 brood per year

Eggs: 5-7; white with brown markings

Incubation: 11-12 days; female incubates

Fledging: 13-14 days; female and male feed young

Migration: non-migrator

Food: insects, seeds; visits seed and suet feeders

Compare: Red-breasted Nuthatch (pg. 219) is smaller with a rust red belly and a distinctive black eye line.

Stan's Notes: The nuthatch's habit of hopping headfirst down tree trunks helps it see insects and insect eggs that birds climbing up the trunk might miss. Incredible climbing agility comes from an extra-long hind toe claw or nail, nearly twice the size of the front toe claws. The name "Nuthatch" comes from the Middle English moniker *nuthak*, referring to the bird's habit of wedging a seed into a crevice and hacking it open. Often seen in flocks with chickadees, Brown Creepers and Downy Woodpeckers. Mated birds will stay with each other year-round, defending small territories. Listen for its characteristic spring call, "whi-whi-whi-whi," given in February and March. One of 17 worldwide nuthatch species.

male

first winter

female

Yellow-rumped Warbler
Setophaga coronata

SUMMER

Size: 5-6" (13-15 cm)

Male: Slate gray with black streaking on the chest. Yellow patches on the rump, flanks and head. White chin and belly. Two white wing bars.

Female: duller than male, but same yellow patches

Juvenile: similar to female

Nest: cup; female builds; 2 broods per year

Eggs: 4-5; white with brown markings

Incubation: 12-13 days; female incubates

Fledging: 10-12 days; female and male feed young

Migration: complete, to southern states, Mexico and Central America

Food: insects, berries; rarely comes to suet feeders

Compare: The Magnolia Warbler (pg. 315) has more yellow. Prairie Warbler (pg. 317) has an olive back with chestnut streaks. The male Yellow Warbler (pg. 313) is yellow with orange streaks on its chest. Palm Warbler (pg. 319) has a yellow throat and chestnut cap. Look for yellow patches on the rump, flanks and head of the Yellow-rumped.

Stan's Notes: Often called Myrtle Warbler in eastern states and Audubon's Warbler in western states. Occasionally called Butter-butts due to the yellow patch on its rump. Familiar call is a single robust "chip," heard mostly during migration. Sings a wonderful song in spring. Male molts to a dull color in winter similar to the female, retaining the yellow patches.

female
pg. 117

male

YEAR-ROUND

Dark-eyed Junco
Junco hyemalis

Size: 5½" (14 cm)

Male: Round, dark-eyed bird with a slate gray-to-charcoal chest, head and back. White belly. Pink bill. Since the outermost tail feathers are white, tail appears as a white V in flight.

Female: same as male, only tan-to-brown color

Juvenile: similar to female, but has a streaked breast and head

Nest: cup; female and male construct; 2 broods per year

Eggs: 3-5; white with reddish brown markings

Incubation: 12-13 days; female incubates

Fledging: 10-13 days; male and female feed young

Migration: complete, across the U.S., non-migrator in New Hampshire and Vermont

Food: seeds, insects; will come to seed feeders

Compare: Rarely confused with any other bird. Small flocks feed under bird feeders in winter.

Stan's Notes: A year-round bird in New Hampshire and Vermont, but usually more commonly seen during winter. Adheres to a rigid social hierarchy, with dominant birds chasing less dominant birds. Look for its white outer tail feathers flashing when in flight. Often seen in small flocks on the ground, where it will "double-scratch" with both feet simultaneously to expose seeds and insects. Eats many weed seeds. Constructs its nest in a wide variety of wooded habitats. Several junco species have now been combined into one, simply called Dark-eyed Junco.

YEAR-ROUND

Tufted Titmouse
Baeolophus bicolor

Size: 6" (15 cm)

Male: Slate gray bird with a white breast and belly. Pointed crest. Flanks are washed with rusty brown. Gray legs and dark eyes.

Female: same as male

Juvenile: same as adult

Nest: cavity; female lines an old woodpecker cavity; 2 broods per year

Eggs: 5-7; white with brown markings

Incubation: 13-14 days; female incubates

Fledging: 15-18 days; female and male feed young

Migration: non-migrator

Food: insects, seeds, fruit; will come to seed and suet feeders

Compare: Closely related to the slightly smaller Black-capped Chickadee (pg. 221), but Titmouse has a crest. Similar size and color as White-breasted Nuthatch (pg. 223), but Nuthatch lacks a crest.

Stan's Notes: Common feeder bird that can be attracted with black oil sunflower seeds. Well known for its quickly repeated "peter-peter-peter" call. The prefix "Tit" comes from a Scandinavian word meaning "little." Suffix "mouse" is derived from the Old English word *mase*, meaning "bird." Simply translated, it is a "small bird." Notorious for pulling hair from sleeping dogs, cats and squirrels to line its nest. Attracted with nest boxes. Usually seen only one or two at a time. Male feeds female during courtship and nesting.

SUMMER

Eastern Phoebe
Sayornis phoebe

Size:	7" (18 cm)
Male:	Gray bird with dark wings, a light olive green belly and thin dark bill.
Female:	same as male
Juvenile:	same as adult
Nest:	cup; female builds; 2 broods per year
Eggs:	4-5; white without markings
Incubation:	15-16 days; female incubates
Fledging:	15-16 days; male and female feed young
Migration:	complete, to southern states and Mexico
Food:	insects
Compare:	Like most other olive gray birds, it is hard to distinguish any identifying markings. Lacks a white eye-ring, but much easier to identify by its well-enunciated "fee-bee" song and characteristic behavior of hawking for insects.

Stan's Notes: Sparrow-sized bird often seen on the end of a dead branch. It sits in wait for a passing insect, flies out to catch it, then returns to the same branch, a process called hawking. Has a habit of pumping its tail up and down when perched. Will build its nest beneath the eaves of a house, underneath a bridge or in culverts. Constructs the nest with mud, grass and moss, and lines it with hair (and sometimes feathers). Common name is derived from its characteristic song, "fee-bee," which it repeats over and over at the top of dead branches.

SUMMER

Great Crested Flycatcher
Myiarchus crinitus

Size: 8" (20 cm)

Male: Gray head with a prominent crest. Gray back and throat with a bright yellow belly; yellow extends under a reddish brown tail. Lower bill is yellow at the base.

Female: same as male

Juvenile: same as adult

Nest: cavity; female and male construct; 1 brood per year

Eggs: 4-6; white or buff with brown markings

Incubation: 13-15 days; female incubates

Fledging: 14-21 days; female and male feed young

Migration: complete, to Mexico and Central America

Food: insects, fruit

Compare: The Eastern Kingbird (pg. 235) has a white band across the tail. Eastern Phoebe (pg. 231) is similar, but it lacks a crest and yellow belly.

Stan's Notes: A common bird of wooded areas in New Hampshire and Vermont. It lives high up in trees, rarely coming to ground. Often heard before seen. The first part of its common name refers to the set of extra-long feathers on top of its head (crest), which the bird raises when alert or agitated, like Northern Cardinals. Feeds by gleaning insects from leaves of trees. Nests in old woodpecker holes but can be attracted to a man-made nest box placed high in a tree, with a 1½-2½-inch (4-6 cm) entrance hole. Often stuffs its nest with a collection of fur, feathers, string and snakeskins. Breeds throughout New Hampshire and Vermont.

233

Eastern Kingbird
Tyrannus tyrannus

SUMMER

Size: 8" (20 cm)

Male: Mostly black gray bird with a white belly and chin. Black head and tail with a distinctive white band across the end of tail. Red crown is concealed and rarely seen.

Female: same as male

Juvenile: same as adult

Nest: cup; male and female build; 1 brood per year

Eggs: 3-4; white with brown markings

Incubation: 16-18 days; female incubates

Fledging: 16-18 days; female and male feed young

Migration: complete, to Mexico, Central America and South America

Food: insects, fruit

Compare: Medium-sized bird, smaller than American Robin (pg. 243). Eastern Phoebe (pg. 231) is smaller and lacks Kingbird's white belly. Look for a white band on the Kingbird's tail.

Stan's Notes: A summer resident seen in open fields. As many as 20 birds migrate together in a group. Returns to the mating ground in spring, where the male and female defend their territory. Acting unafraid of other birds and chasing the larger ones, it is perceived as having an attitude. Its bold behavior gave rise to the common name "King." Perches on tall branches to watch for insects. After flying out to catch them, returns to the same perch–a technique called hawking. Becomes very vocal during late summer, when entire families call back and forth while hunting for insects.

red morph

gray morph

YEAR-ROUND

Eastern Screech-Owl
Megascops asio

Size: 8-10" (20-25 cm); up to 2-foot wingspan

Male: Small "eared" owl that occurs in one of two permanent color morphs: mottled with gray and white or reddish brown (rust) and white. Bright yellow eyes.

Female: same as male

Juvenile: lighter color than adult of the same morph, usually no ear tufts

Nest: cavity, old woodpecker cavity; does not add any nesting material; 1 brood per year

Eggs: 4-5; white without markings

Incubation: 25-26 days; female incubates, male feeds female during incubation

Fledging: 26-27 days; male and female feed young

Migration: non-migrator

Food: large insects, small mammals, birds, snakes

Compare: This is the only small owl in New Hampshire and Vermont with ear tufts. Hard to confuse with its much larger cousin, the Great Horned Owl (pg. 207).

Stan's Notes: A common owl active at dusk and during the night. Excellent hearing and eyesight. Will seldom give a screeching call; more commonly gives a tremulous, descending whiny trill, like a sound effect of a scary movie. Will nest in a wooden nest box. Often seen sunning itself at a nest box hole during the winter. Male and female may roost together at night and are thought to have a long-term pair bond. Different colorations are known as morphs. The gray morph is more common than the red.

male
pg. 293

female

Pine Grosbeak
Pinicola enucleator

WINTER

Size: 9" (22.5 cm)

Female: Plump gray finch with a long dark tail and dark wings. Two white wing bars. Head and rump are tinged dull yellow. Short, stubby, pointed dark bill.

Male: overall rosy red and gray

Juvenile: female is similar to adult female, male has a touch of red on head and rump

Nest: cup; female builds; 1 brood per year

Eggs: 4-5; bluish green without markings

Incubation: 13-15 days; female incubates

Fledging: 13-20 days; female and male feed young

Migration: irruptive; moves around in winter in search of food

Food: seeds, fruit, insects; will come to feeders

Compare: The female Evening Grosbeak (pg. 331) is slightly smaller and lacks the dull yellow head of the female Pine Grosbeak.

Stan's Notes: This finch is common throughout New Hampshire and Vermont in some winters and not so common in others. A very tame and approachable bird. Often seen along roads or on the ground, eating tiny grains of sand and dirt to aid digestion. Seed eater that favors coniferous woods, rarely moving out of coniferous regions in summer. Often seen bathing in fluffy snow. Flies with a typical finch-like undulating pattern while calling a soft whistle. During breeding season, both males and females develop a pouch in the bottom of the mouth (buccal pouch) to transport seeds to their young. Male sings a rich, beautiful song all year.

Gray Catbird
Dumetella carolinensis

SUMMER

Size: 9" (22.5 cm)

Male: Handsome slate gray bird with a black crown and long, thin black bill. Often seen with tail lifted up, exposing a chestnut patch beneath the tail.

Female: same as male

Juvenile: same as adult

Nest: cup; female and male construct; 2 broods per year

Eggs: 4-6; blue green without markings

Incubation: 12-13 days; female incubates

Fledging: 10-11 days; female and male feed young

Migration: complete, to southern states and Mexico

Food: insects, fruit

Compare: Eastern Phoebe (pg. 231) is smaller and has an olive belly. The Eastern Kingbird (pg. 235) has a similar size, but it has a white belly and white tail band.

Stan's Notes: A secretive bird. Chippewa Indians gave it a name that means "the bird that cries with grief" due to its raspy call. The call sounds like the mewing of a house cat, hence the common name. Often mimics other birds, rarely repeating the same phrases. More often heard than seen. Nests in thick shrubs and quickly flies back into shrubs when approached. If a cowbird introduces an egg into a catbird nest, the catbird will quickly break it, then eject it.

male

female

American Robin
Turdus migratorius

YEAR-ROUND
SUMMER

Size: 9-11" (22.5-28 cm)

Male: A familiar gray bird with a rusty red breast and nearly black head and tail. White chin with black streaks. White eye-ring.

Female: similar to male, but with a gray head and a duller breast

Juvenile: similar to female, but has a speckled breast and brown back

Nest: cup; female builds with help from the male; 2-3 broods per year

Eggs: 4-7; pale blue without markings

Incubation: 12-14 days; female incubates

Fledging: 14-16 days; female and male feed young

Migration: complete to non-migrator in New Hampshire and Vermont

Food: insects, fruit, berries, earthworms

Compare: Familiar bird to all.

Stan's Notes: The robin is a complete migrator in northern states, but it's also a year-round resident in most parts of New Hampshire and Vermont. Some don't migrate, spending the winter in low, swampy areas, feeding on leftover berries and insect eggs. Can be heard singing all night in spring. Many people do not realize how easy it is to differentiate between male and female robins. Compare the male's dark, nearly black head and brick red breast with the female's gray head and dull red breast. A robin is not listening for worms moving when cocking its head to one side. It is looking at the earth with its eyes, which are placed far back on the sides of its head. Very territorial, often fighting its own reflection in windows.

displaying

Northern Mockingbird
Mimus polyglottos

YEAR-ROUND

Size: 10" (25 cm)

Male: Silvery gray head and back with a light gray breast and belly. White wing patches, seen in flight or during display. Tail mostly black with white outer tail feathers. Black bill.

Female: same as male

Juvenile: dull gray, a heavily streaked breast, gray bill

Nest: cup; female and male construct; 2 broods per year, sometimes more

Eggs: 3-5; blue green with brown markings

Incubation: 12-13 days; female incubates

Fledging: 11-13 days; female and male feed young

Migration: partial to non-migrator in New Hampshire and Vermont

Food: insects, fruit

Compare: The Gray Catbird (pg. 241) is slate gray and lacks wing patches. Look for Mockingbird to spread its wings, flash its white wing patches and wag its tail from side to side.

Stan's Notes: A very animated bird. Performs an elaborate mating dance. Facing each other with heads and tails erect, pairs will run toward each other, flashing their white wing patches, and then retreat to cover nearby. Thought to flash the wing patches to scare up insects when hunting. Sits for long periods on top of a shrub. Imitates other birds (vocal mimicry), hence the common name. Young males often sing at night. Often unafraid of people, allowing for close observation.

breeding
pg. 57

winter

Black-bellied Plover
Pluvialis squatarola

Size: 11-12" (28-30 cm)

Male: Winter plumage is uniform light gray with dark, nearly black streaks. A white belly and breast. Faint white eyebrow mark. Black legs and bill.

Female: less black on belly and breast than male

Juvenile: grayer than adults, with much less black

Nest: ground; male and female construct; 1 brood per year

Eggs: 3-4; pinkish or greenish, marked with blackish brown splotches

Incubation: 26-27 days; male and female incubate, male incubates during the day, female at night

Fledging: 35-45 days; male feeds young, young learn quickly to feed themselves

Migration: complete, to southeastern New Hampshire, southern states, the Gulf Coast, West Indies, Mexico and Central and South America

Food: insects

Compare: Winter Spotted Sandpiper (pg. 147) has a shorter, thicker bill.

Stan's Notes: Male performs "butterfly" courtship flights to attract females. Female leaves the male and young about 12 days after the eggs hatch. Begins breeding at 3 years of age. A winter resident along coastal New Hampshire and a migrator, seen across New Hampshire and Vermont. During flight, in any plumage, displays a white rump and stripe on the wings with black axillaries (armpits). Often darts across the ground to grab an insect and run.

soaring

juvenile

Sharp-shinned Hawk
Accipiter striatus

YEAR-ROUND
SUMMER

Size: 10-14" (25-36 cm); up to 2-foot wingspan

Male: Small woodland hawk with a gray back and head and rusty red chest. The tail is long with several dark tail bands; widest band is at the end of tail, which is squared. Red eyes.

Female: same as male, only larger

Juvenile: same size as adults, with a brown back and heavily streaked breast, yellow eyes

Nest: platform; female builds; 1 brood per year

Eggs: 4-5; white with brown markings

Incubation: 32-35 days; female incubates

Fledging: 24-27 days; female and male feed young

Migration: partial to non-migrator in New Hampshire and Vermont

Food: birds, small mammals

Compare: The Cooper's Hawk (pg. 257) is larger, has a larger head, slightly longer neck and rounded tail. Red-shouldered Hawk (pg. 183) has a reddish head and belly and lacks a gray back. Look for Sharp-shinned Hawk's squared tail to help identify.

Stan's Notes: Common hawk of backyards and woodlands, often seen swooping in on birds visiting feeders. Its short, rounded wings and long tail allow it to navigate through thick stands of trees in pursuit of prey. Common name comes from the sharp keel on the leading edge of the "shin," although this is actually below (rather than above) the bird's ankle on the tarsus bone of the foot. In most birds, the tarsus is round. In flight, the head doesn't protrude as far as that of the Cooper's Hawk.

Eurasian Collared-Dove
Streptopelia decaocto

YEAR-ROUND

Size: 12½" (32 cm)

Male: Head, neck, chest and belly are pale gray to light tan. A slightly darker back, wings and tail. Black collar with a white border extends around nape of neck. Long squared-off tail.

Female: same as male

Juvenile: similar to adult

Nest: platform; female and male build; 2-3 broods per year

Eggs: 3-5; creamy white without markings

Incubation: 12-14 days; female and male incubate

Fledging: 12-14 days; female and male feed young

Migration: non-migrator

Food: seeds

Compare: Slightly larger and lighter in color than the Mourning Dove (pg. 163). Look for a black collar and squared tail to help identify.

Stan's Notes: A non-native bird. Moved into Florida in the 1980s after introduction to the Bahamas; reached the northern states in the late 1990s. It has been expanding its range across North America and is predicted to spread the same way it did through Europe from Asia. Unknown how this "new" bird will affect the native Mourning Dove. Nearly identical to the Ringed Turtle-Dove, a common pet bird species.

Rock Pigeon
Columba livia

YEAR-ROUND

Size: 13" (33 cm)

Male: No set color pattern. Gray to white, patches of iridescent greens and blues, usually with a light rump patch.

Female: same as male

Juvenile: same as adult

Nest: platform; female builds; 3-4 broods per year

Eggs: 1-2; white without markings

Incubation: 18-20 days; female and male incubate

Fledging: 25-26 days; female and male feed young

Migration: non-migrator

Food: seeds

Compare: Eurasian Collared-Dove (pg. 253) has a black collar. Mourning Dove (pg. 163) is smaller, light brown and lacks all the color variations of the Rock Pigeon.

Stan's Notes: Also known as Domestic Pigeon, formerly known as Rock Dove. Introduced to North America from Europe by the early settlers. Most common around cities and barnyards, where it scratches for seeds. One of the few birds with a wide variety of colors, produced by years of selective breeding while in captivity. Parents feed the young a regurgitated liquid known as crop-milk for the first few days of life. One of the few birds that can drink without tilting its head back. Builds nest underneath bridges and on buildings, balconies, barns and sheds. Was once poisoned as a "nuisance city bird." Many cities now have Peregrine Falcons, which feed on Rock Pigeons, keeping their numbers in check.

soaring

juvenile

Cooper's Hawk
Accipiter cooperii

Size: 14-20" (36-50 cm); up to 3-foot wingspan

Male: Medium-sized hawk with short wings and a long rounded tail with several black bands. Rusty breast and dark wing tips. Slate gray back. Bright yellow spot at base of gray bill (cere). Dark red eyes.

Female: similar to male, only slightly larger

Juvenile: brown back with brown streaks on breast, bright yellow eyes

Nest: platform; male and female construct; 1 brood per year

Eggs: 2-4; greenish with brown markings

Incubation: 32-36 days; female and male incubate

Fledging: 28-32 days; male and female feed young

Migration: complete to non-migrator in New Hampshire and Vermont

Food: small birds, mammals

Compare: Nearly identical to the Sharp-shinned Hawk (pg. 251), only it is larger, darker gray and has a rounded tail.

Stan's Notes: A common resident hawk of woodlands. During flight, look for its large head, short wings and long tail. The stubby wings help it maneuver between trees while pursuing small birds. Comes to feeders, hunting for unaware birds. Flies with long glides followed by a few quick flaps. Known to ambush prey, flying into heavy brush or even running on the ground in pursuit. Nestlings have gray eyes that become bright yellow at 1 year of age and turn dark red later, after 3-5 years.

juvenile

in flight
juvenile

in flight

Peregrine Falcon
Falco peregrinus

MIGRATION
SUMMER

Size: 16-20" (40-50 cm); up to 3¾-foot wingspan

Male: A gray blue back and tail. Breast and under-wings are pale white to tan. Some individuals have a wash of salmon on the breast. Belly, legs, underwings and undertail are covered with small dark spots, looking like horizontal bars. Dark "hood" head marking and a wide black mustache mark. Yellow base of bill, eye-rings and legs.

Female: similar to male, noticeably larger

Juvenile: overall darker than adults, heavy vertical streaks on breast and belly

Nest: ground (scrape), on edge of a cliff; 1 brood per year

Eggs: 3-4; white, occasionally with brown marks

Incubation: 29-32 days; female and male incubate

Fledging: 35-42 days; male and female feed young

Migration: complete, to southern states, Mexico, Central America; some individuals are non-migrators

Food: birds, Rock Pigeons in many cities

Compare: The American Kestrel (pg. 155) is smaller, has two vertical black stripes on its face, and lacks a dark "hood" and mustache mark.

Stan's Notes: A wide-bodied bird of prey often identified by its dark "hood" head marking, clear breast and black mustache mark. Lives and hunts in cities, diving (stooping) on pigeons at speeds up to 200 miles (322 km) per hour. Rural falcons feed on many birds, including shorebirds and waterfowl. Soars with wings flat.

female
pg. 199

male

soaring

Northern Harrier
Circus hudsonius

Size: 18-22" (45-56 cm); up to 4-foot wingspan

Male: A slim, low-flying hawk. Silver gray with a large white rump patch and a white belly. Faint narrow bands across tail. Black wing tips. Yellow eyes.

Female: dark brown back, brown-streaked breast and belly, large white rump patch, narrow black bands across tail, black wing tips, yellow eyes

Juvenile: similar to female, with an orange chest

Nest: ground; female and male construct; 1 brood per year

Eggs: 4-8; bluish white without markings

Incubation: 31-32 days; female incubates

Fledging: 30-35 days; male and female feed young

Migration: complete to partial migrator in New Hampshire and Vermont

Food: mice, snakes, insects, small birds

Compare: Slimmer than the Red-tailed Hawk (pg. 203). Look for black tail bands, a white rump patch and the characteristic flight to help identify.

Stan's Notes: One of the easiest of hawks to identify. Glides just aboveground, following the contours of the land while searching for prey. Holds its wings just above the horizontal position, tilting back and forth in the wind, similar to Turkey Vultures. Formerly called Marsh Hawk due to its habit of hunting over marshes. Feeds on the ground. Will perch on the ground to preen and rest. Unlike other hawks, uses its hearing primarily to locate prey, followed by eyesight. At any age, it has a distinctive owl-like face disk.

in flight

Canada Goose
Branta canadensis

Size: 25-43" (63-109 cm); up to 5½-foot wingspan

Male: Large gray goose with a black neck and head and a white chin or cheek strap.

Female: same as male

Juvenile: same as adult

Nest: platform, on the ground; female constructs; 1 brood per year

Eggs: 5-10; white without markings

Incubation: 25-30 days; female incubates

Fledging: 42-55 days; male and female teach the young to feed

Migration: non-migrator to partial

Food: aquatic plants, insects, seeds

Compare: Large goose that is rarely confused with any other bird.

Stan's Notes: Breeding resident in New Hampshire and Vermont. Formerly killed off (extirpated) in many areas, it was reintroduced and now is common. Begins breeding in the third year, and adults mate for many years. Males frequently act as sentinels, standing at the edge of their group, bobbing their heads up and down, and becoming extremely aggressive to anyone who approaches. Will hiss as though displaying displeasure. Adults molt their primary flight feathers while raising the young, rendering family groups flightless at the same time. Several subspecies vary geographically across the United States; generally they are paler in eastern groups and darker in the West. The size decreases northward, with the smallest subspecies seen on the Arctic tundra.

in flight

Great Blue Heron
Ardea herodias

SUMMER

Size: 42-52" (107-132 cm); up to 6-foot wingspan

Male: Tall gray heron. Black eyebrows extend into several long plumes off the back of head. Long yellow bill. Feathers at the base of neck drop down in a kind of necklace.

Female: same as male

Juvenile: same as adult, but more brown than gray, a black crown and lacks plumes

Nest: platform; male and female construct; 1 brood per year

Eggs: 3-5; blue green without markings

Incubation: 27-28 days; female and male incubate

Fledging: 56-60 days; male and female feed young

Migration: complete, to southern states, Mexico and Central and South America

Food: small fish, frogs, insects, snakes

Compare: Much larger than Green Heron (pg. 271), which has a short, stocky neck and a green back. The Great Egret (pg. 303) is similar in shape, but it has white plumage and is smaller. Look for the long neck and yellow bill of the Great Blue to help identify.

Stan's Notes: One of the most common herons, often barking like a dog when startled. Stalks small fish in shallow water. Strikes at mice, squirrels and just about anything else it may come across. Holds neck in an S shape in flight with its long legs trailing straight out behind, and holds wings in a cupped fashion. Nests in colonies of up to 100 birds. Nests in treetops near or over open water.

Ruby-throated Hummingbird
Archilochus colubris

SUMMER

Size: 3-3½" (7.5-9 cm)

Male: Tiny iridescent green bird. Black throat patch reflects bright ruby red in sunlight.

Female: same as male, but lacking the throat patch

Juvenile: same as female

Nest: cup; female builds; 1-2 broods per year

Eggs: 2; white without markings

Incubation: 12-14 days; female incubates

Fledging: 14-18 days; female feeds young

Migration: complete, to Mexico and Central America

Food: nectar, insects; will come to nectar feeders

Compare: No other bird is as tiny. The Sphinx Moth also hovers at flowers, but it has clear wings and a mouth part that looks like a straw, which coils up when not at flowers. Doesn't hum in flight, moves much slower than the Ruby-throat and can be approached.

Stan's Notes: The smallest bird in New Hampshire and Vermont. Can hover, fly up and down, and is the only bird to fly backward. Does not sing but will chatter or buzz to communicate. The wings create a humming noise, flapping 50-60 times per second or faster during chasing flights. The heart pumps an incredible 1,260 beats per minute, and the bird breathes 250 times per minute. Weighing just 2-3 grams, it takes about five average-sized hummingbirds to equal the weight of one chickadee. Constructs its nest with plant material and spider webs, gluing pieces of lichen on the outside for camouflage. Attracted to tubular red flowers. A long-distance migrator, wintering in the tropics of Central America.

female pg. 189

male

Wood Duck
Aix sponsa

SUMMER

Size: 17-20" (43-50 cm)

Male: A small, highly ornamented dabbling duck with a green head and crest patterned with white and black. Rusty chest, white belly and red eyes.

Female: brown, similar size and shape as male, bright white eye-ring and not-so-obvious crest, blue patch on wing, often hidden

Juvenile: similar to female

Nest: cavity; female lines an old woodpecker cavity; 1 brood per year

Eggs: 10-15; creamy white without markings

Incubation: 28-36 days; female incubates

Fledging: 56-68 days; female teaches young to feed

Migration: complete, to southern states

Food: aquatic insects, plants, seeds

Compare: More colorful than male Green-winged Teal (pg. 171). Lacks the long wide bill of the male Northern Shoveler (pg. 273).

Stan's Notes: Common duck of quiet, shallow backwater ponds. Nearly extinct around 1900 from overhunting but doing well now. Nests in an old woodpecker cavity or uses a nest box. Often seen flying deep in forests or perched high on tree branches. Female takes to flight with a loud squealing call and enters nest cavity from full flight. Lays eggs in a neighboring female nest (egg dumping), resulting in excess of 20 eggs in some clutches. Young stay in nest 24 hours after hatching, then jump from up to 60 feet (18 m) to the ground or water to follow their mother, never returning to the nest.

Green Heron
Butorides virescens

Size: 16-22" (40-56 cm)

Male: Short and stocky heron. Blue-green back and rusty red neck and breast. Dark green crest. Short legs are normally yellow but turn bright orange during breeding season.

Female: same as male

Juvenile: similar to adult, with a blue-gray back and white-streaked chest and neck

Nest: platform; female and male build; 2 broods per year

Eggs: 2-4; light green without markings

Incubation: 21-25 days; female and male incubate

Fledging: 35-36 days; female and male feed young

Migration: complete, to Florida, southern states, Mexico and Central and South America

Food: fish, insects, amphibians, aquatic plants

Compare: Great Blue Heron (pg. 265) is much larger. Look for a small heron with a dark green back and crest stalking the wetlands of New Hampshire and Vermont.

Stan's Notes: Often gives an explosive, rasping "skyew" call when startled. Sometimes it looks like it doesn't have a neck, because it holds its head close to its body. Hunts for small fish, aquatic insects and small amphibians by waiting on the shore or wading stealthily. Places an object, such as an insect, on the water's surface to attract fish to catch. Raises its crest when excited. Nests in a tall coniferous or deciduous tree, often a short distance from the water. Babies give a loud ticking sound, like the ticking of a clock.

female pg. 195

male

MIGRATION
WINTER

Northern Shoveler
Spatula clypeata

Size: 20" (50 cm)

Male: Medium-sized duck with an iridescent green head, rusty sides and white breast. An extraordinarily large, spoon-shaped bill that is almost always held pointed toward the water.

Female: brown and black all over, green speculum, spoon-shaped bill

Juvenile: same as female

Nest: ground; female builds; 1 brood per year

Eggs: 9-12; olive without markings

Incubation: 22-25 days; female incubates

Fledging: 30-60 days; female leads young to food

Migration: complete, to southeastern New Hampshire, southern states, Mexico and Central America

Food: aquatic insects, plants

Compare: Similar to male Mallard (pg. 275), but male Shoveler has a large, characteristic spoon-shaped bill. Larger than male Wood Duck (pg. 269) and lacks the Wood Duck's crest.

Stan's Notes: One of several species of shoveler, so called because of the peculiar shape of its bill. The first part of the common name was given because this is the only species of these ducks in North America. Found in small flocks of 5-10 birds, swimming low in water, pointing its large bill toward the water as if it's too heavy to lift. Feeds mainly by filtering tiny aquatic insects and plants from the surface of the water with its bill, often swimming in tight circles while feeding.

female pg. 197

male

Mallard
Anas platyrhynchos

Size: 19-21" (48-53 cm)

Male: A large, bulbous green head, white necklace and rust brown or chestnut chest. Gray and white on the sides. Yellow bill. Orange legs and feet.

Female: brown duck with an orange and black bill and blue and white wing mark (speculum)

Juvenile: same as female, but with a yellow bill

Nest: ground; female builds; 1 brood per year

Eggs: 7-10; greenish to whitish, unmarked

Incubation: 26-30 days; female incubates

Fledging: 42-52 days; female leads young to food

Migration: partial to non-migrator in New Hampshire and Vermont

Food: seeds, plants, aquatic insects; will come to ground feeders offering corn

Compare: Most people recognize this common duck. The male Northern Shoveler (pg. 273) has a white breast with rust on the sides and a large spoon-shaped bill.

Stan's Notes: A familiar duck of lakes and ponds, it's considered a type of dabbling duck, tipping forward in shallow water to feed on aquatic plants on the bottom. The name "Mallard" comes from the Latin *masculus*, meaning "male," referring to the habit of males not taking part in raising ducklings. Black central tail feathers of male curl upward. Both the male and female have white tails and white underwings. Will return to place of birth.

in flight

female pg. 295

male

Common Merganser
Mergus merganser

SUMMER
WINTER

Size: 27" (69 cm)

Male: Long, thin, duck-like bird with a green head, black back, and white sides, chest and neck. A long, pointed orange bill. Often appears to be black and white in poor light.

Female: same size and shape as the male, but with a rusty red head, ragged "hair" on head, gray body with white chest and chin, and a long, pointed orange bill

Juvenile: same as female

Nest: cavity; female lines an old woodpecker cavity; 1 brood per year

Eggs: 9-11; ivory without markings

Incubation: 28-33 days; female incubates

Fledging: 70-80 days; female feeds young

Migration: partial migrator to complete in New Hampshire and Vermont

Food: small fish, aquatic insects

Compare: Male Mallard (pg. 275) is smaller and lacks the black back and long pointed bill.

Stan's Notes: Can be seen on just about any open water during the winter, but more common along large rivers than lakes. This is a shallow water diver that feeds on fish in 10-15 feet (3-4.5 m) of water. The bill has a fine, serrated-like edge to help catch slippery fish. Females often lay their eggs in nests of other mergansers (egg dumping), resulting in broods of up to 15 young per mother. Male leaves the female as soon as she starts to incubate eggs. Orphans are accepted by other merganser mothers with young.

female
pg. 311

male

American Redstart
Setophaga ruticilla

SUMMER

Size: 5" (13 cm)

Male: A small, striking black bird with contrasting patches of orange on sides, wings and tail. White belly.

Female: olive brown with yellow patches on sides, wings and tail, white belly

Juvenile: same as female, juvenile male attains orange tinges in the second year

Nest: cup; female builds; 1 brood per year

Eggs: 3-5; off-white with brown markings

Incubation: 12 days; female incubates

Fledging: 9 days; female and male feed young

Migration: complete, to Mexico, Central America and South America

Food: insects, seeds, berries rarely

Compare: The male Red-winged Blackbird (pg. 31) and male Baltimore Oriole (pg. 281) are much larger at roughly 8 inches (20 cm). The only small black and orange bird flitting around the top of trees.

Stan's Notes: A common and widespread warbler across New Hampshire and Vermont during summer. Prefers large, unbroken tracts of forest. Appears to be hyperactive when feeding, hovering and darting back and forth to glean insects from leaves. Often droops its wings and fans tail just before launching out to catch an insect. Look for the male's flashing black and orange colors high up in trees.

female pg. 327

male

Baltimore Oriole
Icterus galbula

SUMMER

Size: 7-8" (18-20 cm)

Male: Bright flaming orange bird with a black head and black extending down nape of neck onto the back. Black wings with white and orange wing bars. An orange tail with black streaks. Gray bill and dark eyes.

Female: pale yellow with orange tones, gray brown wings, white wing bars, gray bill, dark eyes

Juvenile: same as female

Nest: pendulous; female builds; 1 brood per year

Eggs: 4-5; bluish with brown markings

Incubation: 12-14 days; female incubates

Fledging: 12-14 days; female and male feed young

Migration: complete, to Mexico, Central America and South America

Food: insects, fruit, nectar; will come to orange half and nectar feeders

Compare: The male Orchard Oriole (pg. 283) is much darker orange than the flaming orange male Baltimore Oriole. The male American Redstart (pg. 279) is much smaller and has more black than orange.

Stan's Notes: A fantastic songster, this bird is often heard before seen. Easily attracted to a feeder offering grape jelly, orange halves or sugar water (nectar). Parents bring their young to feeders. Sits in treetops, feeding on caterpillars. Female builds a sock-like nest at the outermost branches of tall trees. Often returns to the same area year after year. Seen during migration and summer. Some of the last birds to arrive in spring and first to leave in fall.

female
pg. 329

male

first-year
male

Orchard Oriole
Icterus spurius

SUMMER

Size: 7-8" (18-20 cm)

Male: Dull orange oriole with a black head, chin, wings and tail, and black extending down the back. Single white wing bars. Long, thin black bill with a small gray mark on lower mandible (jaw).

Female: olive green back with a dull yellow belly, two white wing bars on dark gray wings

Juvenile: same as female, black bib on first-year male

Nest: pendulous; female builds; 1 brood per year

Eggs: 3-5; pale blue to white, brown markings

Incubation: 11-12 days; female and male incubate

Fledging: 11-14 days; female and male feed young

Migration: complete, to Mexico, Central America and northern South America

Food: insects, fruit; visits fruit and nectar feeders

Compare: Similar to male Baltimore Oriole (pg. 281), but male Orchard Oriole has a much darker orange body.

Stan's Notes: Prefers orchards or open woods, hence its common name. Eats insects until wild fruit starts to ripen. Summer resident in southern parts of New Hampshire and Vermont. Often nests alone; sometimes nests in small colonies. Parents bring their young to orange half and jelly feeders right after they fledge. Many people think the orioles have left the area during summer, but the birds are just concentrating on finding insects to feed their young. Often migrates with Baltimore Orioles.

male

female
pg. 109

yellow
male

House Finch
Haemorhous mexicanus

YEAR-ROUND

Size: 5" (13 cm)

Male: An orange red face, breast and rump, with a brown cap. Brown marking behind the eyes. Brown wings streaked with white. A white belly with brown streaks.

Female: brown with a heavily streaked white chest

Juvenile: similar to female

Nest: cup, occasionally in a cavity, female builds; 2 broods per year

Eggs: 4-5; pale blue, lightly marked

Incubation: 12-14 days; female incubates

Fledging: 15-19 days; female and male feed young

Migration: non-migrator to partial; will move around to find food

Food: seeds, fruit, leaf buds; will visit seed feeders

Compare: Male Purple Finch (pg. 287) is very similar, but male House Finch lacks the red crown. Look for the streaked breast and belly, and brown cap of the male House Finch.

Stan's Notes: Very social, visiting feeders in small flocks. Can be the most common bird at feeders. Likes to nest in hanging flower baskets. Male sings a loud, cheerful warbling song. House Finches that were originally introduced to Long Island, New York, from the western U.S. in the 1940s have since populated the eastern U.S. Although relatively new to New Hampshire and Vermont, they are now found across the country. Male feeds the incubating female. Suffers from a fatal eye disease that causes the eyes to crust. Rarely, some males are yellow (see inset), probably due to poor diet.

female
pg. 125

male

Purple Finch
Haemorhous purpureus

YEAR-ROUND

Size: 6" (15 cm)

Male: A raspberry red head, cap, breast, back and rump. Brownish wings and tail.

Female: heavily streaked brown and white bird with large white eyebrows

Juvenile: same as female

Nest: cup; female and male build; 1 brood per year

Eggs: 4-5; greenish blue with brown markings

Incubation: 12-13 days; female incubates

Fledging: 13-14 days; female and male feed young

Migration: non-migrator to partial in New Hampshire and Vermont; moves around during winter to find food

Food: seeds, insects, fruit; comes to seed feeders

Compare: Redder than the orange red of male House Finch (pg. 285), with a clear breast. Male House Finch has a brown cap unlike the male Purple Finch's red cap.

Stan's Notes: A year-round resident throughout New Hampshire and Vermont, and New Hampshire's state bird. Travels in flocks of up to 50 individuals. Visits seed feeders along with House Finches, making it hard to tell them apart. Feeds mainly on seeds, with ash tree seeds an important source of food. Prefers open woods or woodland edges. Sings a rich, loud song, giving a distinctive "tic" note only in flight. Not a purple color, the Latin species name *purpureus* means "crimson" or other reddish color.

female
pg. 325

male

SUMMER

Scarlet Tanager
Piranga olivacea

Size: 7" (18 cm)

Male: A bright scarlet red bird with jet-black wings and tail. Ivory bill and dark eyes.

Female: drab greenish yellow bird with olive wings and tail, whitish wing linings, dark eyes

Juvenile: same as female

Nest: cup; female builds; 1 brood per year

Eggs: 4-5; blue green with brown markings

Incubation: 13-14 days; female incubates

Fledging: 9-11 days; female and male feed young

Migration: complete, to Central and South America

Food: insects, fruit

Compare: Male Northern Cardinal (pg. 291) has a black mask and red bill and lacks the black wings of male Scarlet Tanager.

Stan's Notes: This is a tropical-looking bird that prefers mature, unbroken woodlands, where it hunts for insects high at the top of trees. Requires at least 4 acres (1.5 ha) for nesting; prefers 8 acres (3 ha). It arrives late in spring and leaves early in fall. Male sheds (molts) its bright red plumage in the fall, appearing more like the female. Scarlet Tanagers are included in some 240 tanager species in the world. Nearly all are brightly colored and live in the tropics. The common name "Tanager" comes from a South American Tupi Indian word meaning "any small, brightly colored bird."

female
pg. 149

male

juvenile

Northern Cardinal
Cardinalis cardinalis

YEAR-ROUND

Size: 8-9" (20-22.5 cm)

Male: All-red bird with a black mask that extends from the face down to the chin and throat. Large red bill and crest.

Female: buff brown with tinges of red on crest and wings, same black mask and red bill

Juvenile: same as female, but with a blackish gray bill

Nest: cup; female builds; 2-3 broods per year

Eggs: 3-4; bluish white with brown markings

Incubation: 12-13 days; female and male incubate

Fledging: 9-10 days; female and male feed young

Migration: non-migrator

Food: seeds, insects, fruit; comes to seed feeders

Compare: The male Scarlet Tanager (pg. 289) has black wings and tail. Look for the male Northern Cardinal's black mask, large crest and red bill.

Stan's Notes: A familiar backyard bird. Look for the male feeding the female during courtship. Male feeds young of the first brood by himself while the female builds a second nest. The name comes from the Latin word *cardinalis*, which means "important," as represented by Catholic cardinals in their scarlet priestly garments. Very territorial in spring, it fights its own reflection in a window or other reflective surface. Non-territorial during winter, gathering in small flocks of up to 20 birds. Both the male and female sing and can be heard anytime of year. Listen for its "whata-cheer-cheer-cheer" territorial call in spring.

male

female
pg. 239

Pine Grosbeak
Pinicola enucleator

WINTER

Size: 9" (22.5 cm)

Male: Plump rosy red and gray finch with a long dark tail. Dark wings with a smattering of gray. Two white wing bars. A short, stubby, pointed dark bill.

Female: mostly gray with dark wings and tail, head and rump are tinged dull yellow

Juvenile: male has a touch of red on head and rump, female is similar to adult female

Nest: cup; female builds; 1 brood per year

Eggs: 4-5; bluish green without markings

Incubation: 13-15 days; female incubates

Fledging: 13-20 days; female and male feed young

Migration: irruptive; moves around in winter in search of food

Food: seeds, fruit, insects; will come to feeders

Compare: Male Purple Finch (pg. 287) and male House Finch (pg. 285) are much smaller.

Stan's Notes: This finch is common throughout New Hampshire and Vermont in some winters and not so common in others. A very tame and approachable bird. Often seen along roads or on the ground, eating tiny grains of sand and dirt to aid digestion. Seed eater that favors coniferous woods, rarely moving out of coniferous regions in summer. Often seen bathing in fluffy snow. Flies with a typical finch-like undulating pattern while calling a soft whistle. During breeding season, both males and females develop a pouch in the bottom of the mouth (buccal pouch) to transport seeds to their young. Male sings a rich, beautiful song all year.

in flight

male pg. 277

female

Common Merganser

Mergus merganser

SUMMER
WINTER

Size: 27" (69 cm)

Female: A long, thin, duck-like bird with a rusty red head and ragged "hair" on the back of head. Gray body with white chest and chin. Long, pointed orange bill.

Male: same size and shape as the female, but with a green head, black back, white sides and chest, and long, pointed orange bill

Juvenile: same as female

Nest: cavity; female lines an old woodpecker cavity; 1 brood per year

Eggs: 9-11; ivory without markings

Incubation: 28-33 days; female incubates

Fledging: 70-80 days; female feeds young

Migration: partial migrator to complete in New Hampshire and Vermont

Food: small fish, aquatic insects

Compare: Hard to confuse with other birds. Look for ragged "hair" on back of a red head, a long, pointed orange bill, white chest and chin.

Stan's Notes: Can be seen on just about any open water during the winter, but more common along large rivers than lakes. This is a shallow water diver that feeds on fish in 10-15 feet (3-4.5 m) of water. The bill has a fine, serrated-like edge to help catch slippery fish. Females often lay their eggs in nests of other mergansers (egg dumping), resulting in broods of up to 15 young per mother. Male leaves the female as soon as she starts to incubate eggs. Orphans are accepted by other merganser mothers with young.

in flight

breeding

juvenile

winter

Ring-billed Gull
Larus delawarensis

Size: 19" (48 cm); up to 4-foot wingspan

Male: A white bird with gray wings, black wing tips spotted with white, and a white tail, as seen in flight. Yellow bill with a black ring near the tip. Yellowish legs and feet. Winter or non-breeding adult has a speckled brown back of head and nape of neck.

Female: same as male

Juvenile: brown speckles with a brown tip of tail and a mostly dark bill

Nest: ground; female and male construct; 1 brood per year

Eggs: 2-4; off-white with brown markings

Incubation: 20-21 days; female and male incubate

Fledging: 20-40 days; female and male feed young

Migration: partial migrator to complete in New Hampshire and Vermont

Food: insects, fish; scavenges for food

Compare: Herring Gull (pg. 299) has an orange-red mark on its lower bill, pink legs and lacks a black ring on its bill. Great Black-backed Gull (pg. 75) has a black back and orange spot on its lower bill.

Stan's Notes: A common gull of garbage dumps and parking lots. This bird is expanding its range and remaining farther north longer during winter due to successful scavenging in cities. A three-year gull with different plumages in its first three fall seasons. Attains the ring on bill after its first winter and adult plumage in the third year. Defends a small area around nest, usually a few feet.

in flight

breeding

winter

juvenile

Herring Gull
Larus argentatus

YEAR-ROUND
MIGRATION
WINTER

Size: 23-26" (58-66 cm); up to 5-foot wingspan

Male: Snowy white bird with slate gray wings and black wing tips with tiny white spots. Bill is yellow with an orange-red spot near the tip of lower bill. Pinkish legs. Winter plumage head and neck are dirty gray to brown.

Female: same as male

Juvenile: uniformly mottled brown to gray, black bill

Nest: ground; female and male construct; 1 brood per year

Eggs: 2-3; olive with brown markings

Incubation: 24-28 days; female and male incubate

Fledging: 35-36 days; female and male feed young

Migration: partial migrator to complete in New Hampshire and Vermont

Food: fish, insects, clams, eggs, baby birds

Compare: Larger than Ring-billed Gull (pg. 297), which has yellowish legs, a black ring near the tip of its bill and lacks the orange-red spot on its lower mandible.

Stan's Notes: Common gull of large lakes and along the coast. An opportunistic bird, scavenging for food from dumpsters, but will also take other birds' eggs and young right from the nest. Often drops clams and other shellfish from heights to break shells and get to the soft interior. Nests in colonies, returning to the same site year after year. Lines its ground nest with grasses and seaweed. It takes about four years for juveniles to obtain adult plumage. Adults molt to dirty gray in winter and look similar to the juveniles.

white
morph

blue morph

juvenile

in flight

Snow Goose
Anser caerulescens

MIGRATION

Size: 25-38" (63-96 cm); up to 4½-foot wingspan

Male: A mostly white goose with varying patches of black and brown. Black wing tips. Pink bill and legs. Some individuals are grayish with a white head.

Female: same as male

Juvenile: overall dull gray with a dark bill

Nest: ground; female builds; 1 brood per year

Eggs: 3-5; white without markings

Incubation: 23-25 days; female incubates

Fledging: 45-49 days; female and male teach the young to feed

Migration: complete, to southern states and Mexico

Food: aquatic insects and plants

Compare: The Mute Swan (pg. 305) is much larger, lacks black wing tips and has a prominent black knob on the base of its bill. The Canada Goose (pg. 263) has a black neck and white chin strap.

Stan's Notes: This bird has two color morphs. The more common white morph is pure white with black wing tips. The gray morph, often called blue, has a white head, gray chest and back, and pink bill and legs. Its thick, serrated bill helps to pull up plants. Breeds in large colonies on the northern Canadian tundra. Females begin breeding at 2-3 years. Older females produce more eggs and are more successful than the younger females. Seen by the thousands during migration.

in flight

Great Egret
Ardea alba

Size: 38" (96 cm); up to 4½-foot wingspan

Male: Tall, thin, elegant all-white bird with a long, pointed yellow bill. Black stilt-like legs and black feet.

Female: same as male

Juvenile: same as adult

Nest: platform; male and female construct; 1 brood per year

Eggs: 2-3; light blue without markings

Incubation: 23-26 days; female and male incubate

Fledging: 43-49 days; female and male feed young

Migration: complete, to southern states, Mexico and Central America

Food: fish, aquatic insects, frogs, crayfish

Compare: Smaller than the Great Blue Heron (pg. 265), but similar in shape.

Stan's Notes: A tall and stately bird, the Great Egret slowly stalks shallow wetlands looking for small fish to spear with its long sharp bill. Nests in colonies of up to 100 individuals. Now protected, it was hunted to near extinction in the 1800s and early 1900s for its long white plumage to decorate women's hats. The common name "Egret" comes from the French *aigrette*, meaning "ornamental tufts of plumes." The plumes grow near the tail during breeding season.

YEAR-ROUND

Mute Swan
Cygnus olor

Size: 60" (152 cm); up to 7-foot wingspan

Male: Completely white bird. Holds its neck in an S shape with bill pointed toward the surface of water. Large orange bill with a prominent black knob at the base.

Female: same as male

Juvenile: brown-to-gray bird, gray bill with a black base, bill lacks a prominent knob

Nest: ground; female and male construct; 1 brood per year

Eggs: 4-8; light gray without markings

Incubation: 35-40 days; female and male incubate

Fledging: 115-150 days; female and male feed young

Migration: non-migrator; will move to areas with open water during winter

Food: aquatic insects and plants

Compare: Hard to confuse with other birds. Look for a long-necked white bird with a large orange bill and prominent black knob on the face.

Stan's Notes: Usually silent, not mute. Makes a variety of sounds, including hisses, barks and snorts when agitated. An introduced species, frequently in lakes, parks, zoos, golf courses and private property, now found in the wild. Often swims with wings arched over its back. Neck is always held in an S shape. Uses neck to reach plants on lake or pond bottom. Forms a long-term pair bond. Pairs defend large territories, driving off any other large birds including native swans and geese. Some states work to reduce the number of Mute Swans because of the fear of competition with native species.

winter male

male

female

American Goldfinch
Spinus tristis

YEAR-ROUND

Size: 5" (13 cm)

Male: Perky yellow bird with a black patch on the forehead. Black tail and a conspicuous white rump. Black wings with white wing bars. No marking on the breast. A dramatic change in color during winter, similar to female.

Female: dull olive yellow with brown wings and white rump, lacks a black forehead

Juvenile: same as female

Nest: cup; female builds; 1 brood per year

Eggs: 4-6; pale blue without markings

Incubation: 10-12 days; female incubates

Fledging: 11-17 days; female and male feed young

Migration: partial to non-migrator; small flocks of up to 20 birds move around North America

Food: seeds, insects; will come to seed feeders

Compare: The male Yellow Warbler (pg. 313) is yellow with orange streaks on the chest. Pine Siskin (pg. 107) has a streaked chest and belly and yellow wing bars. The female House Finch (pg. 109) and Purple Finch (pg. 125) have heavily streaked chests.

Stan's Notes: A common backyard resident year-round, moving around to find adequate supplies of food during winter. Most often in open fields, scrubby areas and woodlands. Enjoys Nyjer seed in feeders. Breeds in late summer, using the silky down from wild thistle for its nest. Appears roller-coaster-like in flight. Listen for it to twitter during flight. Almost always in small flocks. Often called Wild Canary.

male

female

SUMMER

Common Yellowthroat
Geothlypis trichas

Size: 5" (13 cm)

Male: Olive brown bird with a bright yellow throat and breast, white belly and distinctive black mask outlined in white. A long, thin, pointed black bill.

Female: similar to male, lacks the black mask

Juvenile: same as female

Nest: cup; female builds; 2 broods per year

Eggs: 3-5; white with brown markings

Incubation: 11-12 days; female incubates

Fledging: 10-11 days; female and male feed young

Migration: complete, to southern states, Mexico and Central America

Food: insects

Compare: Male Yellow Warbler (pg. 313) has orange streaks on its chest and lacks the mask of the male Yellowthroat. Found in a similar habitat as American Goldfinch (pg. 307), but lacks the male's black forehead and wings. Yellow-rumped Warbler (pg. 225) only has patches of yellow compared with the bright yellow breast of the Yellowthroat.

Stan's Notes: A common warbler of open fields and marshes. Has a cheerful, well-known song, singing "witchity-witchity-witchity-witchity" from deep within tall grasses. Nests low to the ground in a simple cup nest. The male performs a curious courtship display, bouncing in and out of tall grass while uttering an unusual song. The young remain dependent on their parents longer than most other warblers. A frequent cowbird host.

male
pg. 279

female

American Redstart
Setophaga ruticilla

Size: 5" (13 cm)

Female: Olive brown with yellow patches on sides, wings and tail. White belly.

Male: small, striking black bird with contrasting patches of orange on sides, wings and tail, white belly

Juvenile: same as female, juvenile male attains orange tinges in the second year

Nest: cup; female builds; 1 brood per year

Eggs: 3-5; off-white with brown markings

Incubation: 12 days; female incubates

Fledging: 9 days; female and male feed young

Migration: complete, to Mexico, Central America and South America

Food: insects, seeds, berries rarely

Compare: Similar to the female Yellow-rumped Warbler (pg. 225), but lacks a yellow patch on rump.

Stan's Notes: A common and widespread warbler across New Hampshire and Vermont during summer. Prefers large, unbroken tracts of forest. Appears to be hyperactive when feeding, hovering and darting back and forth to glean insects from leaves. Often droops its wings and fans tail just before launching out to catch an insect. Look for the male's flashing black and orange colors high up in trees.

Yellow Warbler
Setophaga petechia

SUMMER

Size: 5" (13 cm)

Male: Yellow warbler with orange streaks on the chest and belly. Long, pointed dark bill.

Female: same as male, but lacks orange streaking

Juvenile: similar to female, only much duller

Nest: cup; female builds; 1 brood per year

Eggs: 4-5; white with brown markings

Incubation: 11-12 days; female incubates

Fledging: 10-12 days; female and male feed young

Migration: complete, to Mexico, Central America and South America

Food: insects

Compare: Yellow-rumped Warbler (pg. 225) has just spots of yellow unlike the orange streaks on the yellow chest of male Yellow Warbler. Male American Goldfinch (pg. 307) has a black forehead and wings. Female Yellow Warbler is similar to the female American Goldfinch (pg. 307), but it lacks white wing bars.

Stan's Notes: Resident warbler during summer in New Hampshire and Vermont, seen in gardens and shrubby areas near water. A prolific insect eater, gleaning small caterpillars and other insects from tree leaves. Male is usually seen higher up in trees than the female. Female is less conspicuous. Begins to migrate south in August; returns in late April. Males arrive 1-2 weeks before females to claim territories. Migrates at night in mixed flocks of warblers. Rests and feeds during the day.

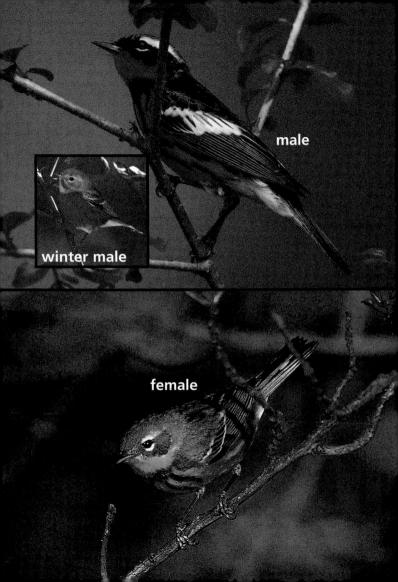

male

winter male

female

SUMMER

Magnolia Warbler
Setophaga magnolia

Size: 5" (13 cm)

Male: Yellow and black warbler with a gray crown and white eyebrows. Heavy black streaks on a yellow chest and belly. White wing patch. Yellow rump. Obvious white patches on tail.

Female: similar to male, lacks black on the face, has two white wing bars

Juvenile: same as female

Nest: cup; female and male build; 1 brood per year

Eggs: 3-5; white with brown markings

Incubation: 11-13 days; female incubates

Fledging: 8-10 days; female and male feed young

Migration: complete, to Central America

Food: insects

Compare: More yellow than the Yellow-rumped Warbler (pg. 225). The Yellow Warbler (pg. 313) lacks black on the face and a black back.

Stan's Notes: This is a common warbler during summer, nesting in New Hampshire, Vermont, other northern states and Canada. Populations are stable due to the ability to adapt to second-growth forest. Look for it low in trees, where it feeds on insects. Often fans its tail while picking insects from undersides of leaves. Males often feed higher up in trees than the females. Named "Magnolia" when ornithologist Alexander Wilson saw the species in a magnolia tree.

Prairie Warbler
Setophaga discolor

MIGRATION
SUMMER

Size: 5" (13 cm)

Male: Bright yellow from chin to belly. Olive back with chestnut-colored streaks. Black streaks on the sides from the neck down. Black line through eyes. Yellow eyebrows.

Female: same as male, only duller

Juvenile: similar to female

Nest: cup; female builds; 2 broods per year

Eggs: 3-5; white with brown markings

Incubation: 11-14 days; female incubates

Fledging: 8-11 days; female and male feed young

Migration: complete, to the Caribbean

Food: insects

Compare: The Magnolia Warbler (pg. 315) has more black than the Prairie Warbler. The Yellow Warbler (pg. 313) lacks any black. The male Common Yellowthroat (pg. 309) has a black mask. Watch for Prairie Warbler to twitch its tail when feeding.

Stan's Notes: A common warbler during migration and summer in the southern half of New Hampshire and Vermont. Returns in mixed flocks of warblers in late April to mid-May. Named "Prairie" when it was first found in a barren area in Kentucky, but this was a misnomer because it has nothing to do with prairies. Nests in dry, brushy clearings and forest edges, making it the perfect host for Brown-headed Cowbirds. Will sometimes desert a parasitized nest. Nests in an upright fork of a tree. Feeds young mainly caterpillars.

Palm Warbler
Setophaga palmarum

MIGRATION

Size: 5½" (14 cm)

Male: Distinctive yellow eyebrows. A yellow throat, belly and undertail. An obvious chestnut cap. Thin chestnut streaks on the sides of breast. Dark line across dark eyes.

Female: same as male

Juvenile: same as adult, but duller and brown

Nest: cup; female builds; 1-2 broods per year

Eggs: 4-5; white with brown markings

Incubation: 11-12 days; female incubates

Fledging: 12-13 days; female and male feed young

Migration: complete, to southeastern states, West Indies, Central America

Food: insects, fruit

Compare: Yellow-rumped Warbler (pg. 225) has a similar size, but lacks the yellow throat and belly of the Palm. The Pine Warbler (pg. 321) has pronounced white wing bars. Look for the yellow eyebrows and chestnut cap of the Palm Warbler.

Stan's Notes: A migrant warbler in New Hampshire and Vermont, seen in backyard woodlands. Look for it to wag or bob its tail while gleaning insects from leaves and flowers of trees. One of the few warblers to feed on the ground. Hops rather than walks. Nests at the edges of northern spruce bogs. Recognizes cowbird eggs and destroys them, burying them with its nest, which it builds on top of the cowbird nest.

Pine Warbler
Setophaga pinus

Size: 5½" (14 cm)

Male: A yellow throat and breast with faint black streaks on sides of breast. Olive green back. Two white wing bars. White belly.

Female: similar to male, only paler

Juvenile: similar to adults, browner with more white on belly

Nest: cup; female builds; 2-3 broods per year

Eggs: 3-5; white with brown markings

Incubation: 10-12 days; female incubates

Fledging: 12-14 days; female and male feed young

Migration: complete, to southern states

Food: insects, seeds, fruit

Compare: Palm Warbler (pg. 319) is similar, but it has a chestnut cap and yellow eyebrows; the Pine Warbler has much more pronounced white wing bars than the Palm. The Yellow-rumped Warbler (pg. 225) has yellow patches on its rump. American Goldfinch (pg. 307) lacks streaks on its breast.

Stan's Notes: Summers in the pine forests of New Hampshire and Vermont. Builds its nest only in pine woods. Brighter in spring and more drab in fall, it varies in color depending upon the time of year. Thought to have a larger bill than any of the other warblers. Sometimes easier to identify by its song than by sight. Listen for a twittering, musical song that varies in speed.

female

male
pg. 23

Bobolink
Dolichonyx oryzivorus

SUMMER

Size: 7" (18 cm)

Female: Pale yellow bird with dark brown stripes on the head. Thin dark line extends through the eye. Dark streaks on back and sides.

Male: nearly all-black bird with pale yellow on back of head and nape of neck, white patch on wings and rump

Juvenile: similar to female, lacking dark streaks

Nest: ground; scraped-out depression lined with grass; 1 brood per year

Eggs: 4-6; gray to red brown with brown markings

Incubation: 10-13 days; female incubates

Fledging: 10-14 days; female and male feed young

Migration: complete, to South America, mostly Brazil

Food: insects, seeds

Compare: Smaller than Eastern Meadowlark (pg. 333) and lacks the obvious black V marking on the breast. Smaller and more yellow than the female Red-winged Blackbird (pg. 151), with dark brown stripes on its head.

Stan's Notes: A member of the blackbird family. Closely related to meadowlarks. A common bird of prairies, grasslands and open fields. In spring, the male will perch on plant stems and repeat its bubbling "bob-o-link" song (which provided the common name). Gives a loud, repeated "ink" whistle during flight. When disturbed, the female will run from her highly concealed ground nest before taking flight. By late summer, the males will have molted to a drab color similar to the females.

female

male
pg. 289

Scarlet Tanager
Piranga olivacea

SUMMER

Size:	7" (18 cm)
Female:	Drab greenish yellow bird with olive wings and tail. Whitish wing linings. Dark eyes.
Male:	bright scarlet red bird with jet-black wings and tail, ivory bill and dark eyes
Juvenile:	same as female
Nest:	cup; female builds; 1 brood per year
Eggs:	4-5; blue green with brown markings
Incubation:	13-14 days; female incubates
Fledging:	9-11 days; female and male feed young
Migration:	complete, to Central and South America
Food:	insects, fruit
Compare:	Female Baltimore Oriole (pg. 327) has gray brown wings and white wing bars. Female American Goldfinch (pg. 307) is smaller and has white wing bars.

Stan's Notes: This is a tropical-looking bird that prefers mature, unbroken woodlands, where it hunts for insects high at the top of trees. Requires at least 4 acres (1.5 ha) for nesting; prefers 8 acres (3 ha). It arrives late in spring and leaves early in fall. Male sheds (molts) its bright red plumage in the fall, appearing more like the female. Scarlet Tanagers are included in some 240 tanager species in the world. Nearly all are brightly colored and live in the tropics. The common name "Tanager" comes from a South American Tupi Indian word meaning "any small, brightly colored bird."

male pg. 281

female

Baltimore Oriole
Icterus galbula

Size: 7-8" (18-20 cm)

Female: A pale yellow bird with orange tones, gray brown wings, white wing bars, a gray bill and dark eyes.

Male: bright flaming orange bird with a black head and black extending down nape of neck onto the back, black wings with white and orange wing bars, an orange tail with black streaks, gray bill and dark eyes

Juvenile: same as female

Nest: pendulous; female builds; 1 brood per year

Eggs: 4-5; bluish with brown markings

Incubation: 12-14 days; female incubates

Fledging: 12-14 days; female and male feed young

Migration: complete, to Mexico, Central America and South America

Food: insects, fruit, nectar; will come to orange half and nectar feeders

Compare: The female Orchard Oriole (pg. 329) is very similar, but it lacks orange tones and has less pronounced wing bars.

Stan's Notes: A fantastic songster, this bird is often heard before seen. Easily attracted to a feeder offering grape jelly, orange halves or sugar water (nectar). Parents bring their young to feeders. Sits in treetops, feeding on caterpillars. Female builds a sock-like nest at the outermost branches of tall trees. Often returns to the same area year after year. Seen during migration and summer. Some of the last birds to arrive in spring and first to leave in fall.

male
pg. 283

female

first-year
male

SUMMER

Orchard Oriole
Icterus spurius

Size: 7-8" (18-20 cm)

Female: An olive green bird with a dull yellow belly. Two white wing bars on dark gray wings. Long, thin black bill with a small gray mark on lower mandible (jaw).

Male: dull orange with a black head, chin, upper back, wings and tail, single white wing bars

Juvenile: same as female, black bib on first-year male

Nest: pendulous; female builds; 1 brood per year

Eggs: 3-5; pale blue to white, brown markings

Incubation: 11-12 days; female and male incubate

Fledging: 11-14 days; female and male feed young

Migration: complete, to Mexico, Central America and northern South America

Food: insects, fruit; visits fruit and nectar feeders

Compare: Female Baltimore Oriole (pg. 327) is similar, but it has orange tones and more distinct wing bars. Female Scarlet Tanager (pg. 325) is mustard yellow with a larger bill.

Stan's Notes: Prefers orchards or open woods, hence its common name. Eats insects until wild fruit starts to ripen. Summer resident in southern parts of New Hampshire and Vermont. Often nests alone; sometimes nests in small colonies. Parents bring their young to orange half and jelly feeders right after they fledge. Many people think the orioles have left the area during summer, but the birds are just concentrating on finding insects to feed their young. Often migrates with Baltimore Orioles.

male

juvenile

female

Evening Grosbeak
Coccothraustes vespertinus

Size: 8" (20 cm)

Male: A striking bird with a stocky body, a large ivory-to-greenish bill and bright yellow eyebrows. Dirty yellow head, yellow rump and belly and black-and-white wings and tail.

Female: similar to male, with softer colors and a gray head and throat

Juvenile: similar to female, with a brown bill

Nest: cup; female builds; 1 brood per year

Eggs: 3-4; blue with brown markings

Incubation: 12-14 days; female incubates

Fledging: 13-14 days; female and male feed young

Migration: irruptive; moves around New Hampshire and Vermont during winter in search of food

Food: seeds, insects, fruit; comes to seed feeders

Compare: Larger than its close relative, the American Goldfinch (pg. 307). The female Evening Grosbeak is slightly smaller than the female Pine Grosbeak (pg. 239) and has a gray head. Look for the dark head, bright yellow eyebrows and large thick bill to identify the male Evening Grosbeak.

Stan's Notes: One of the largest finches. Characteristic undulating finch-like flight. An unusually large bill for cracking seeds, its main food source. Often seen on gravel roads eating gravel, from which it gets minerals, salt and grit to grind the seeds it eats. Sheds the outer layer of its bill in spring, exposing a blue green bill. Moves in flocks in winter, searching for food, often coming to feeders. More numerous in some years than others. Sometimes totally absent.

Eastern Meadowlark
Sturnella magna

YEAR-ROUND SUMMER

Size: 9" (22.5 cm)

Male: A robin-shaped bird with a yellow breast and belly, brown back and prominent V-shaped black necklace. White outer tail feathers.

Female: same as male

Juvenile: same as adult

Nest: cup, on the ground in dense cover; female builds; 2 broods per year

Eggs: 3-5; white with brown markings

Incubation: 13-15 days; female incubates

Fledging: 11-12 days; female and male feed young

Migration: complete to non-migrator in New Hampshire and Vermont

Food: insects, seeds

Compare: Horned Lark (pg. 135) is smaller and lacks a yellow breast and belly. Look for a black V marking on the breast to help identify the Eastern Meadowlark.

Stan's Notes: A bird of open grassy country. Named "Meadowlark" because it's a bird of meadows and sings like the larks of Europe. Best known for its wonderful song–a flute-like, clear whistle. Often seen perching on fence posts but quickly dives into tall grass when approached. It has conspicuous white markings on each side of its tail, most often seen when flying away. Nest is occasionally domed with dried grass. Not a member of the lark family, it actually belongs to the blackbird family and is related to grackles and orioles. Overall population is down greatly due to intensive agricultural activities and ditch mowing.

HELPFUL RESOURCES

New Hampshire and Vermont Birding Hotlines

To report unusual bird sightings or possibly hear recordings of where birds have been seen, you can often call pre-recorded hotlines detailing such information. Since these hotlines are usually staffed by volunteers, and phone numbers and even the organizations that host them often change, the phone numbers are not listed here. To obtain the numbers, go to your favorite internet search engine, type in something like "rare bird alert hotline New Hampshire" or "rare bird alert hotline Vermont" and follow the links provided.

Web Pages

The internet is a valuable place to learn more about birds. You may find birding on the net a fun way to discover additional information or to spend a long winter night. These websites will assist you in your pursuit of birds. If a web address doesn't work (they often change a bit), just enter the name of the group into a search engine to track down the new web address.

Site	Address
New Hampshire Audubon	www.nhaudubon.org/get-outside/birding
Audubon Vermont	vt.audubon.org
American Birding Association	www.aba.org
Cornell Lab of Ornithology	www.birds.cornell.edu
Author Stan Tekiela's home page	www.naturesmart.com

CHECKLIST/INDEX BY SPECIES

Use the boxes to check the birds you've seen.

OTHER BOOKS & PRODUCTS FOR THE NORTHEAST BY STAN

Field Guides

Birds of Connecticut Field Guide
Birds of Maine Field Guide
Birds of Maryland & Delaware Field Guide
Birds of Massachusetts Field Guide
Birds of New Jersey Field Guide
Birds of New York Field Guide
Birds of Pennsylvania Field Guide
Birds of Prey of the Northeast Field Guide
Trees of New York Field Guide
Trees of Pennsylvania Field Guide

Audio CDs

Birds of Maryland & Delaware Audio CDs
Birds of New York Audio CDs
Birds of Pennsylvania Audio CDs
Bird Songs of the Northwoods:
    Soothing Sounds of Nature Series Audio CD
Fascinating Loons: Alluring Sounds of the Common Loon Audio CD

Nature Books

A Year in Nature with Stan Tekiela: A Naturalist's Notes on the Seasons
Bird Nests: Amazingly Ingenious and Intricate
Feathers: A Beautiful Look at a Bird's Most Unique Feature
Our Love Of Loons

Backyard Bird Feeding Guides

Cardinals
Finches
Hummingbirds
Orioles

Quick Guides

Birds of the Northeast

Appreciation Book Series

Amazing Hummingbirds: Unique Images and Characteristics
Bears: Black, Brown & Polar Bears
Captivating Bluebirds: Exceptional Images and Observations
Cranes, Herons & Egrets: The Elegance of Our Tallest Birds
Deer, Elk & Moose: Grand and Majestic Creatures
Fascinating Loons: Amazing Images & Behaviors
Intriguing Owls: Exceptional Images and Insight
Majestic Eagles: Compelling Facts and Images of the Bald Eagle
Remarkable Woodpeckers: Incredible Images and Characteristics
The Lives of Wolves, Coyotes and Foxes

Children's Books

Baby Bear Discovers the World
C is for Cardinal
Critter Litter
Do Beavers Need Blankets?
Some Babies Are Wild
The Cutest Critter
Whose Butt?

Board Book Series

Floppers & Loppers
Paws & Claws
Peepers & Peekers
Snouts & Sniffers

Wildlife Puzzles

Goldfinch in the Garden
Gray Wolf Eyes
Moose at the Mountains
Red-bellied Woodpecker

Playing Cards

Birds of the Northeast
Mammals of the Northeast
Trees of the Northeast

ABOUT THE AUTHOR

Naturalist, wildlife photographer and writer Stan Tekiela is the originator of the popular state-specific field guide series that includes *Birds of Maine Field Guide*. Stan has authored more than 190 educational books, including field guides, quick guides, nature books, children's books, playing cards and more, presenting many species of animals and plants.

With a Bachelor of Science degree in Natural History from the University of Minnesota and as an active professional naturalist for more than 30 years, Stan studies and photographs wildlife throughout the United States and Canada. He has received various national and regional awards for his books and photographs. Also a well-known columnist and radio personality, his syndicated column appears in more than 25 newspapers, and his wildlife programs are broadcast on a number of Midwest radio stations. Stan can be followed on Facebook and Twitter. He can be contacted via www.naturesmart.com.